Spiritually Fulfilled

A Poetry Collection

By Shaista Hussain

2019

Preface

This is a collection of deep poetry written on a whole plethora of issues, ideas and beliefs. Some are from my personal experiences and insights; others are based on my analysis and observation of others.
We are all travellers on a spiritual path seeking our destinies hence this book is an odyssey into a journey of a huge proportion of the world's population.

Hopefully these poems will enlighten the reader to delve into the deepness of these issues and benefit.

Shaista Hussain

2019

Acknowledgements

Glory and all praise to Allah the Lord of the worlds and Majesty for blessing me with the ability to complete this endeavour.

Salutations to Muhammad (p.b.u.h) whose life, Sunnah (example) and teachings inspired this.

I offer my gratitude to all the good people mentioned within this book for inspiring me to write about them. I offer my gratitude also to those who taught and inspired me with knowledge that I have articulated through poetry. I dedicate this to the above and to all of my nieces and nephews whose love is ever dear to me.

© 2019 by Shaista Hussain (ilm82) All rights are reserved. No part of this book may be reproduced or transmitted in any shape or by any means, electronic or mechanical, including photocopying or recording or by any information storage and retrieval system without permission in writing from the author.

Contents:

	Page
Introduction	*6-7*

Chapter 1

Marhaba (Welcome)	8
The author's Journey	9
Test	10

Chapter 2

Hadith I Jibrail	*11*
Iman – The six beliefs	12
The 99 names of Allah (Asma ul Husna)	13-16
Malaikah (Angels)	17
Holy Books	18
The noble Qur'an	19
Risalah (Prophethood)	20
Yawm ul Qiyamah (Day of Judgement)	21
Qadr	22
Qadr	23

Chapter 3

Islam	24
The Shahadah (Declaration)	25
Salah – The Prayer	26
Zakah – The Charity	27
Sawm – Fasting in Ramadan	28
Ramadan	29
Preparing on a journey	30
Hajj	31
Rejuvenated	32

Chapter 4

Ihsan	33
Ihsan	34

Chapter 5

Allah	35
Alhamdulillah	36
Allah's blessings	37

Chapter 6

The Prophets	38
Yaqub (Jacob) (a.s) & Yusuf (Joseph) (a.s)	39-41
Musa (a.s)	42
Mariam (r.a) and Isa (a.s)	43-44
Muhammad (pbuh) A Mercy to Mankind	45-52
Blessed Prophet	53
Muhammad (pbuh) A Mercy to Mankind 2	54

Chapter 7
Islam's path to success — 55

Islam	56
Consumption with the love of faith	57
The Teachers	58
Champions	59
The Right path	60
The faith most dear	61

Chapter 8
Deep Thinking — 62-64

Allah's existence	65
My perfect world	66
Questions	67
Inspiration	68
The Rose – the majesty of the garden	69
Miraculous stars	70
The child & the Sages - reflective help from the Wise	71-74
Irreplaceable	75
God vs Satan	76
The Sky	77

Chapter 9
Women in Islam — 78-81

Women of success	82
The veil	83
Hijab	84
Mother	85
Precious mother	86

Chapter 10
Marriage-Love-Divorce — 87-88

Marriage – Zawj	89
Completing half of faith	90
My love, My spouse	91
An ode from a Queen to her King	92
Types of Ishq	93
Divorce most hated	94

Chapter 11
Along the Journey of life and death — 95

Loving child – Praises from mothers	96
Little miracles – Blessings in disguise	97
An ode to Tahir	98
Little innocent child	99
By your side my friend	100
Death	101
Muslim Eschatology – signs before Qiyamah	102
Eschatology	103
Akhira	104
Jannah (Heaven)	105
Jahannam (Hell)	106-107

Chapter 12
Peace & Justice vs War — 108

The occupiers	109
Palestine	110
Palestine – I hear your cry	111
Syria & Burma	112
War child	113
Poverty	114
We know	115
Peace	116
Forgiveness	117

Chapter 13
The Vision — 118

A child's dream	119-120
Education	121
Education for the future	122

Chapter 14
Reflections on the times — 123

Tough Times	124
Racism – Goodbye, farewell!	125
Racism – say no and taste the rainbow!	126
Smoking – It's harmful I'm not joking	127
Drugs – don't risk it!	128
Gangsters	129
Islamophobia	130
Think Twice	131
Not ashamed to be different	132

Chapter 15
Others — 133

Tears	134
Gratitude	135
An ode of appreciation	136
Thank you	137
Healing	138
The world of Trials	139
The Sojourner	140
The Awakenings	141

Chapter 16
Remembrance & Supplication — 142

Remembrance	143
A Muslim Dua (Supplication)	144
Dua	145

Conclusion	146
Appendix 1	147
Appendix 2	148
Glossary	149-151

Introduction

Poetry is an art and language of its own. Its pen is the heart and its ink is the feeling and emotions inherent within it. Poetry expresses words that cannot be expressed in conversation alone, but through an amalgamation of language using rhythm and different styles to express some of the most sentimental of values, ideas and experiences as well as the thoughts of the poet. Poetry is not an ordinary form of writing for the poet, but is inspired or written with greater meaning then the words written that can express a whole plethora of ideas and values. Poetry certainly exhibits the ideal of writing beyond script and for entertainment, but to extend to those parts of humans that go beyond the five senses.

I have always exhibited deep thought since an early age where my thought was deep, spiritual and very inquisitive of the world and experiences I underwent. This journey was expressed through what I saw, felt literally and metaphorically, heard, experienced, and encountered. There were many nights when sleep was absent as the thinker within me fought and debated as both the protagonist and antagonist of the very questions my mind emerged with, such deep thought helped me reach my final conclusions on matters perennial in my spiritual development.

Religion was not coerced upon me, but was a waterfall with which I became imbued and flowed with its water and stream to become fulfilled. The questions that were not answerable by other means found themselves answered by Islam. The insecurities or injustices I saw could not be explained by the foolish type of reason absent of faith as they served no foundational values alone. Hence the truth was to be searched and an in depth study of religious ideas and secular ideologies were taken. To compliment this, I was lucky to have numerous encounters with people of divergent beliefs or no beliefs with who conversations and interaction served beneficial for me to develop my own thinking and mind-set. This path helped me to journey on the road of trepidation, and difficulties to find an answer and to become confident in an intellectual system that provided me the edifice for my existence and to know that the penultimate conclusion is: Faith is requisite to aid, guide, enhance and ensure that we are *spiritually fulfilled* as this book is aptly titled.

Spiritual sojourners never end their journey, for every day they traverse the path in their own development, fulfilment and enhancement. The path we tread on is filled with trials and trepidations, joys and sorrows, happiness and sadness, life and death – realities we reflect on and need to understand on a deeper level. But most importantly spiritual sojourners wish to build and develop their connection with the One that has bestowed them with the blessing they have, that is Allah The Most Merciful, The Most Compassionate, and The Lord of the Worlds with the most beautiful of names. This Dhikr – Remembrance & Glorification and enumeration of blessings helps develop the connection both in this world and to reap its rewards in the next.

In life many of us live in a world of imagination, forgetting to comprehend the unique signs before our eyes. The complexity within the world and beyond reality should baffle us, for despite the little two eyes we have the world before us is uniquely designed with a complexity that reaches beyond the five senses. Yet if we move beyond a limited periscope of thinking to matters beyond, we start to see the unravelling of things greater and consequently allowing for greater opportunities within our own minds and manifest in our lives. This book really has asset of thematic sections that we can infer from, develop and move forward with like a traveller who seeks to find his/her destination – hopefully along the route some of the keys may be found within the book.

The book is filled with summations & connections on enlightening matters, matters of faith and issues that bind us all, or that we all on our journey of life encounter. Furthermore, in some cases the poems and sections really are exhorting the reader to think and reflect and ponder to aid them to the final conclusions that become self-evident throughout the text. I hope that any shortcomings in here are overlooked with the finite nature of my existence.

The book is not comprised of language alone but converses with the reader on some of the most salient issues and experiences that we encounter. It primarily is an introduction to the Islamic faith but also to issues faced by all. In some cases it answers deep questions, in some cases it provides a summation of perennial ideas and beliefs and in other cases articulates thoughts and experiences and values common to us all whatever our religious affiliation or disposition. I hope it aids the reader on their journey of thought and their search for spiritual fulfilment.

To aid the reader I have included a glossary at the end. I would advise the reader to read through the glossary either whilst reading the book or before to comprehend the language used in the book if they are unfamiliar with terms. It generally does not include words bracketed or explained in the main text.

With Truth, Peace, Justice & Harmony

Shaista Hussain

Marhaba (Welcome)

Welcome reader to spiritually fulfilled,
I hope you enjoy the read as I willed.

You may have had this book to you gifted,
After the read I hope it will have uplifted.

Or you may have read it out of intrigue,
Inspired by poetry & those of league.

Each opener will have pre-judgements,
But will leave with their own sentiments.

The book explores Islam and many issues,
It endeavours to enlighten and you imbues.

It is a book that upon you does not coerce,
It is filled with differing styles and verse.

It is a book of poems to be enjoyed,
Many issues are covered not to avoid.

Read the book open-minded and treat it well,
Reflect on this book and journey that I tell.

The author's journey

Upon a spiritual path I wish to traverse,
No compulsion on the reader of this verse.
I have become more recently to faith inclined,
Focusing on my heart, body and the mind.

Be prepared for the journey of life,
For some it comes with ease & others strife.
Tested are we upon our walk and way,
To each our deeds what we do and say.

Tests and trials we endure and we feel,
But to these we have the path that will heal.
To destruction and turmoil don't be confined,
Travel on the path as God is Most Kind.

Human wrong and mistakes many make,
But to the world of trials stay awake.
The seeker wishes to learn and enhance,
Life is short for everyone only one chance.

Spiritually fulfilled with Islam & words,
To fly with wings stretched like birds.
No longer to be imprisoned in cages,
To sit and learn from the righteous sages.

Freedom from hell & wrong for the soul,
Faith in Islam is the route for me to extol.
The hold of God's antithesis Satan I'll break,
My faith is firm it's all after I die I'll take.

I endeavour to be in glorification of my Lord,
I have not been forced it's of my accord.
I shall now travel with faith as my luggage,
With pearls of faith I won't need to rummage.

I wish to succeed and My Maker knows,
His Light is immense and on humans glows.
The Qur'an is from He who all of us made,
He enjoined good and wrong He forbade.

Test

Born into this world – ahead is the test,
From innocence to account in life's quest.
Tribulations & tests to be won & to be fought,
From the way of the Prophet & what was sought.

Good doers gain if not in this world the next,
Deep & perennial is the need for emulation of text.
Text of the Qur'an & the Sunnah to be guided,
Choices we make were known in Qadr decided.
Decided by the writ of what you decided & know,
Utilising Aql, right niyyah & nur will in you glow.

Success is determined on exertion to do right,
You take the step forward & the rest is led by light.
Light shining, empowering as a blessing & gift,
No matter the throw & fall faith will give a lift.

Tested by wealth & those upon whom it's spent,
To remember it's an amanah - use it for what it's meant.
As with your life for which the test requires account,
To lead it upright so the good deeds on mizan amount.

Blessings already exist in the test for much gratitude,
Shukr to Allah will have you all in faith imbued.
It requires praise & appreciation from right attitude,
On the path of faith Taqwa is the uplift in latitude.

Tests will not always be what we deem to be fair,
Those around you may test for intent please be aware.
Those around you are tested on how they respond & care,
To God is the final account whose law is always fair.

When tested it's easy to give up & to despair,
This is the wish of God's foe beware his lair.
Since God made you all with in mind a special design,
So you remember that the blessings around you are divine.

The test of the innocent is not of account to an age,
As of the mentally disabled, God decides their page.
Since no account is on them as with those who are Shaheed,
As with mothers in childbirth and babies that die in their need.

The test will be used in deciphering your final fate,
The words of the Qur'an and the hadith this state.
Humans have a divinely ordained purpose to live,
So be upright and God fearing if you want Him to forgive.

Hadith I Jibrail

The Hadith I Jibrail alludes to an encounter Muhammad (pbuh) had with the angel Jibrail whilst he was with his companions. He showed no signs of travelling and was clothed in white. The angel postulates five questions to him. The first is "what is Islam?" the second "what is Iman?" and the third "what is Ihsan?" the fourth is "Tell me about the Hour" and finally the fifth is "Tell me about its signs."

To the first question about Islam the Prophet responds that this is:

- Testification of faith
- Perform prayers
- Pay Zakah
- Fast in Ramadan
- Make pilgrimage (Hajj)

To the second question about Iman the Prophet responds that this is belief in:

- Allah
- His angels
- His books
- His Messengers
- The last day
- Divine destiny – its good and bad

To the third question about Ihsan the Prophet responded that this is:

"It is to worship Allah as though you see Him, and if you do not see Him, then (knowing that) truly He sees you."

To the fourth question about the Hour the Prophet stated that the questioned knows no more than the questioner. Since this was considered the reserve knowledge of Allah.

To the fifth question about its signs the Prophet gave some examples of the signs.

In the section on Iman I have written poems on all aspects of Iman outlined above. In the section on Islam I have written poems on all aspects of Islam outlined above. In the section on Ihsan I have written a poem that elaborates on the above. Also, in the section on the journey of life and death I have written a poem on some of the Signs before the Day of Judgment.

As this hadith is important I thought it would be beneficial to basically elaborate on the elements outlined in this beautiful hadith.

Iman – The six beliefs

- Belief in God (1)
- Belief in Angels (2)
- Belief in God's Revealed Books (3)
- Belief in the Messengers of God (4)
- Belief in the Day of Judgment (5)
- Belief in pre-destination (6)

The Six pillars of Faith
"Basic Islamic Beliefs"

The 99 names of Allah (Asma ul Husna)

Muslims believe Allah has 99 names beautiful,
To Him we should fully submit & be dutiful.

A task with which I feel inside quite smitten,
Here includes a poem on 99 names I have written.

Allah created the world and all He is Al-Khaliq,
King of Kings He is above all and is Al-Malik

He has salient Light in completeness An-Nur,
He is patient with humanity and all As-Sabur.

His signs and systems in the world show Az-Zahir,
He is Al-Awwal the beginning and final as Al-Akhir.

Perfect Wisdom is His manifest in Qur'an Al-Hakim,
He bestows upon us countless bounties His Al-Karim.

He gives rewards but also abases as He is Al-Khafid,
He can bring things back to original form Al-Mu'id.

He is the best of Judges for Judgement Al-Hakam,
He is kind and He is the King Dhul-Jalal Wa'l Ikram.

He is the giver of perfect revelation & guidance Al-Hadi
Everything created emanates from Him Al-Badi.

Glory, praise and submission belong to Him Al-Majid,
He is unique and not in need of anyone Al-Wajid.

He fashioned everything as He desired Al-Musawwir,
His Prevalent over everything that happens Al-Muqtadir.

He Hears everything no limit of distance As-Sami,
He is the sovereign that elevates as He pleases Ar-Rafi.

He confers on His creation bounties & blessings Al-Wahhab,
He accepts remorse & forgives from His Mercy At-Tawwab.

He is the trusted and the One whom entrusts Al-Wakil,
He lowers and trials as to His Will Al-Mudhill.

His forgiveness is infinite & a sign of His Mercy Al-Ghaffar,
He is above all & dominates everything He made Al-Qahhar.

He is brilliant, fantastic and amazing Al-Mutakabir,
He delays matters to their appointed times Al-Muakhir.

You cannot resist Him since He is magnificent Al-Jabbar,
He is benevolent and shows His benevolence Al-Barr.

He has complete power and mightiness He is Al-Aziz,
He honours amongst what He makes Al-Muizz.

He protects what His made from many harms Al-Muhaymin,
Peace and tranquillity are bestowed by Him Al-Mu'min.

He transcends time and space He is infinite As-Samad,
Tawhid professes He has no equal and is One namely Al-Ahad.

Glorious and lofty by self is He Al-Muta'ali,
He protects and guards from harm Al-Wali.

He forwards things to what is His accord Al-Muqaddim,
He has infinite mercy and confers this to us Ar-Rahim.

Without Him we have nought He provides Ar-Razzaq,
All goodness and truth manifest in Him Al-Haqq.

He has the greatest testimony as the seer Ash-Shahid,
He does not beget neither was He Begotten Al-Wahid.

He is secure and firmness belongs to Him Al-Matin,
He knows everything's innermost He is Al-Batin.

He is generous and kind and gives kindly He is Al-Barr,
He distresses gives trials and tribulations Ad-Darr.

He has permanence no beginning or end Al-Baqi,
He shows favour and promise and propriety An-Nafi.

He enriches, enhances and gives increases Al-Mughni,
He suffices for Himself and has no dependency Al-Ghani.

He is the one that made everything as He is Al-Bari,
On Judgement day He will gather all Al-Jami.

He appreciates all good endeavours & acts Ash-Shakur,
He pardons and forgives sins of humanity Al-Ghafur.

He seizes and takes back as He pleases Al-Qabid,
He deserves all praise and prayers Al-Hamid.

He guides aright humanity into light Ar-Rashid,
All Praise and Glory belongs to him Al-Majeed.

Glory and praise is His to His greatness Al-Kabir,
He has knowledge & awareness of all Al-Khabir.

He has full capability and has no limits Al-Qadir,
His sight prevails the ordinances of all Al-Basir.

He responds to prayers and the universe Al-Mujib,
He has no limit to His sight and sees over everything Ar-Raqib,
He is the one that will reckon all at a time Al-Hasib.

His knowledge has no limits or boundaries Al-Aleem,
He is compassionate and generous to us Al-Halim,
He is the One to whom greatness belongs Al-Azeem.

Death is given at His discretion Al-Mumit,
He is a perfect Judge of Justice He is Al-Muqsit.
He maintains the universe & everything Al-Muqit.

He created and gave life to everyone Al-Muhyi,
He is the one that began and found all Al-Mubdi,
He counts all from his infinite knowledge Al-Muhsi.

He is magnificent, awe-inspiring and amazing Al-Aliy,
He is the benefactor & supporter of the truth Al-Waliy,
He is the Lord Most High that also exalts Ar-Rafi.

Sanctimoniously higher and holy and pure He is Al-Quddus,
He who follows His path of success will never lose.

He subsists lives and exists by Himself Al-Qayyum,
He exists as signs are evident we don't assume.

He is the giver of harmony & amity and is As-Salam
He is the one to trust as He protects from Harm.

His power & strength has no limitation Al-Qawi,
The Creator of the great Bukhari, Muslim & Nawawi.

He lives and subsists and will never die Al-Hayy,
He knows our innermost and everything we say.

The greatest kingdom He has as His Malik ul Mulk.
His names and their magnitude amazingly bulk.

He is the gentlest & takes care of all detail Al-Rauf,
Of Him have Tawakkul, Yaqeen, Taqwa and hauf.

He pardons and forgives us our manifest sins Al-Afuw,
From the Qur'an and Hadith about Him we know.

He avenges and has the power over all as Al-Muntaqim,
His light (nur) is Everlasting and will never dim.

Ownership and inheritance in total is His Al-Warith
He owns all that we have and all that we bequeath.

He has Hudud (boundaries) and prevents Al-Mani,
He rewards humans and Jinn who are very Imani.

He is the protector and guards His dominion Al-Hafiz,
He is the Lord independent & does as He so please.

He is kind and goodness is His Al-Latif,
He takes out of difficulty and gives relief.

He is sovereign & perfectly Just as Al-Adl,
His divine justice one cannot wrong or muddle.

He gives life, death & will resurrect all Al-Ba'ith.
He loves the steadfast on the path of faith.

He is caring and loving to all His creation Al-Wadud,
The signs of his existence are clear so don't feud.

He shows His creation compassion as Ar-Rahman,
He loves those who are firm on Islam & iman.

He embraces in fullness He is Al-Wasi,
Hater of tyrannies if it be that of Pharaoh or a Nazi.

Glory belongs to Him Most High Al-Jalil,
He gave Islam a religion for a just deal.

He opens all possibilities and goodness Al-Fattah,
He is none other than The One who is Allah.

It has been narrated by Abu Hurairah (r.a) that Allah's Messenger (pbuh) said:
"Verily Allah (SWT) has ninety-nine names, hundred but one, he who memorises them will enter Paradise." (Bukhari & Muslim)

Malaikah (Angels)

Malaikah are made from pure light,
They are obedient to Allah and do right.

They unlike humans do not have free-will,
In Allah's praise & glorification is their fill.

Malaikah are appointed & given tasks,
They do as Allah pleases, whatever He asks.

The angels - Messengers of Allah are they,
To Allah they submit, worship and pray.

They have a variety of different roles,
And for being dutiful everyone extols.

Carrying Allah's throne is the Hamalat al 'Arsh,
Blessed like all – they are gentle not harsh.

Jibrail is the deliverer of divine revelation,
He is a messenger of lofty elevation.

The angel of Mercy is known as Mikail,
He submits to Allah without any fail.

Israfil will commence the end of time,
Mentioned in Akhira another rhyme.

Azrail the angel of death appears,
Gentle or harsh your happiness or fears.

The Kiraman Katibeen take your account,
On your shoulders writing deeds that amount.

Munkar & Nakir will question in the grave,
3 questions answered by the rightful brave.

Zabaniyah are the angels that punish in hell,
They are appointed by Allah as well.

Malik is the chief of angels in the abode hell,
The Zabaniyah do as Allah and Malik does tell.

Dardaiyl looks for those remembering Allah,
In gatherings of remembrance wallah.

Ridwan is responsible for the abode Jannah,
Unto him is a blissful place & a great amanah.

Holy Books

Muslims believe in Holy books God given,
To challenges of the time that had arisen.
But also as books of guidance and light,
To help people decipher wrong and right.

They believe that they were all divine writ,
Protected in Heaven each & every bit.
They are protected in the Lahw al Mahfuz,
Preserved in original so none can confuse.

Allah gave Ibrahim (pbuh) Suhuf or Leaves,
He was an upright friend of God that believes.
It is not existent & longer to be found by us,
But in the preserved Tablet protected thus.

Allah gave Musa (pbuh) the Holy book Torah,
Written in Hebrew a book of wonder and aura.
It was given to guide his people the Hebrews,
It was Moses on Sinai and in Egypt that He chose.

Allah gave Dawud (pbuh) the Zabur (Psalms),
Words of praise that rejoice and truly calms.
It was a book of Hikmah also known as wisdom,
Given to a King who has his own kingdom.

Allah gave Isa (pbuh) the book called Injil,
To a Prophet who the lepers et al would heal.
It was given as a book to guide all the Jews,
It was a revelation & from God the Good News.

These revelations were altered or changed,
From the original they were rearranged.
People over time added new additions,
No longer the given Prophetic missions.

Allah gave Muhammad (pbuh) the Qur'an,
It is a book of criterion called the Furq'an.
It was given as a guidance for every nation,
It's preserved and leads to spiritual liberation.

The revelation given is called in Arabic Wahi,
The same given to every single Ukhti and Akhi.
The books were sent with purpose to guide,
To follow Allah's commands & laws abide.

The noble Qur'an

The Qur'an is the final revelation,
Held in esteem and much elevation.
From the words of Allah its emanation,
Sent as a miracle to this nation.

Its words are the most beautiful,
It exhorts us to be good and dutiful.
The book teaches the straight path,
It's the route for mercy and not wrath.

It was given as a miracle & blessing,
Its words are so truly enveloping.
It contains Surahs that are a total 114,
It is the way of Islam a complete deen.

Sent to Muhammad (p.b.u.h) complete,
Its words are guarded non can compete.
A revelation of unique prose and poetry,
Given to the chosen Prophet; the finality.

It was given to the Prophet by Jibrail,
It is a book of shifa and does heal.
It is amongst other books Allah did reveal,
Such as Torah, Zabur, Suhuf and the Injil.

The first revelation was in cave Hira,
To the beloved of Allah most dearer.
It has and still withstands the test of time,
A remarkable book considered sublime.

Preserved in lahw al Mahfuz by Allah,
It teaches obedience in the salah.
Written in Arabic language of heaven,
Layers of which there are seven.

It was sent as a completed guide,
For us to follow and devotedly abide.
Sent over a period of 23 years,
About all people it helps and cares.

It has 30 chapters (juz), that in its divided,
It is perfect as Allah's Kalam as He decided.
It is a book memorised by so many peeps,
To be guarded and saved safe where it keeps.

The first word of the Qur'an was to read,
It teaches Taqwa and Allah's laws to heed.
It was first given on the Night of Power,
Following it is every Muslims endeavour.

It contains over 6000 ayahs or verses in it,
It is completely divinely infallible every bit.
To Judge it is the criterion known as Furqan,
It teaches the path of Islam, Ihsan & iman

It is the primary source of Islamic law,
Free of blemish or any type of flaw.
It is an untainted source of authority,
It guides to heaven and the path of piety.

Those who commit it to memory are Hafiz,
Or hafizah with Tawwakul it comes with ease.
Recited in prayers and many occasions,
It brings solace and positive sensations.

A book of guidance and illumination,
A blessing to the Prophet's nation.
It teaches the route of true liberation,
It guides to heavenly emancipation.

"This is the Scripture in which there is
no doubt, containing guidance for those
who are mindful of God." (Qur'an 2:2)

"This is truly a glorious Qur'an (written)
on a preserved Tablet." (Qur'an 85:21-22)

Risalah (Prophethood)

A Prophet was sent to every societal nation,
To remove ignorance & give emancipation.
Teaching was their prime God-given occupation,
Success was to be through their imitation.

The Prophets faced trials and tribulation,
Their goal was of disbelief its elimination.
They were obedient and gave God elevation,
Guided by God and not personal insinuation.

The Qisas al Ambiyah are Prophetic stories,
Accounting God's given wonders & His glories.
They are found in the holy book the Qur'an,
It alludes to their lives and firmness in iman.

All of the Prophetic missions taught Tawhid,
They were warner's, who taught people to heed.
They were men of kindness and not greed,
They were pure in lineage & righteous seed.

There were in history a total of 124,000,
They were followers of Allah's command.
Avoiding shirk they would all equally demand,
They were shepherds to their flock on land.

The Prophets mentioned in Qur'an are 25,
Many of their trials in time still survive.
Their messages and Prophecies were alive,
They warned that transgressors connive.

The Prophets tried to abolish age old idolatry,
The practice is polytheism in our contemporary.
They warned of hell and punishments scary,
They taught that shirk to Tawhid is contrary.

Their prophecies portents of future foretell,
They wished for the best and had meant well.
They wished to protect from the fire of hell,
And guide to Heaven and goodness as well.

They were chosen for righteousness & piety,
They solely worshipped God & no other deity.
They were men of heaven & foresight in entirety.
They taught patience and virtue and rid of anxiety.

First and foremost they were all of law teachers,
They imbued and guided their nation as preachers.
They taught protection of earth and all creatures,
Their messages in our times still fully features.

Each of them were assigned by God this quest,
They taught this life is the withstanding test.
They worked arduously to the task & had little rest,
Guided by Allah they knew what was the best.

The Prophets gave to God their full submission,
Often they endured ridicule, mock & derision.
They were men for God their sole role & mission,
They had foresight, prophecy, miracles and vision.

Many of them saw the archangel called Jibrail,
From God he gave revelation to the Prophet's seal.
Each of them for their purpose had passion & zeal,
Often from their people rejection they would feel.

313 were messengers called nabi who were chosen,
124,000 were Prophets called rasul who were golden.
They came to past nations to guide in days olden,
But the messages remain for today and still embolden.

They were the finest exemplars, upright & saliheen,
They spoke what God would want & were siddiqeen,
They were steadfast and firmly unwavering on deen,
Blessed are the miracles and footsteps they have been.

Yawm ul Qiyamah (Day of Judgement)

To commence Angel Israfil will blow a Ram's horn,
Non after this can do anything or weep or mourn.
On Angel Israfil's the first blowing all things will die,
He is only subservient to His Creator Allah most High.
2nd blowing is the human resurrection to plain of Arafat,
Humans will rise again as though new is their heart.
3rd blowing all humans will be judged on their deeds,
Success will be to those who Allah's law in life heeds.

Whilst standing at Arafat they will be unclothed,
Too fearful to worry on this day to God deeds are owed.
There will be no shade except the shade of Allah only,
For the steadfast protected from the sun for being holy.
For the good in their right hand will be a book of deeds,
For the bad in their left hand will be a book of deeds.
Each in their life had two angels taking their account,
On this day they will be judged for what is their amount.

All deeds will be weighed on the (Mizan) balance,
Once the judgement takes place there is no chance.
Once the deeds are weighed there will be a (Sirat) bridge,
Those who were good will cross it with utmost courage.
They will cross it and end up in the abode of Heaven,
Those who fall enter hell of which there are seven.
The bridge is thinner than hair & sharper than a sword,
Only by deeds is the corollary not personal accord.

The Prophet that day will intercede for his community,
Though just being Muslim will not be an immunity.
Since upon our deeds as Muslims were held account,
We need to be good to receive Kawthar the fount.

Qadr

Qadr of future events is God's foreknowledge,
In the 'Iman ay Mufassal' Muslims this acknowledge.
Conceptually it is also called predestination,
Taught about by the Prophet to his Muslim nation.

Allah in the Lahw al Mahfuz has a record of our fate,
It is a preserved tablet that no one can eliminate.
Everything that happens is by His Divine decree,
But we have choice penultimate to this we are free.

Muslims believe Allah is All-Knowing as Al-Aleem,
He knows our fate thus but we don't, He is Al-Hakim.
Allah gave us free-will to ponder & make choices,
We choose ourselves what we do with action & voices.

Allah knows all of what is in everyone's destiny,
However our choices mean there is accountability.
Thus the existence of the places of Heaven & Hell,
After judgement, then in either abode we may dwell.

Humans had Prophets, who gave a purpose & plan,
From free-will for each to do whatever they can.
Their teachings were embedded in the divine law,
That taught Allah judges on choices without any flaw.

Laws existed because of free-will to teach us morality,
We cannot then blame God for human immorality.
Since His All-knowing and knows all our decisions,
He sent Prophets of Ihsan with sacred types of visions.

Even though Allah knows we make our own intention,
The devil might mislead and make foolish mention.
Nevertheless, we have nafs (instincts) to still choose,
If we trust Allah and His guidance we will not lose.

In Allah we must have belief, yaqeen and full trust,
Humans are finite so it is an imperative given must.
God gave each and everyone a mind with which to think,
Beware the devil and his guile in his trap don't sink.

Humans must beware the sin of believing in fatalism,
The belief we have no choice is like a type of schism.
Since Allah's foreknowledge is in the 99 names,
The rest is the devil at play so beware his games.

Judgement day would not exist if we had no free-will,
Our life is a test with guidance so of Allah don't think ill.
You must follow the Qur'an and Sunnah and it will fulfil.
In your children & yourselves good choices try to instill.

Qadr 2

Trust the one who knows your fate,
Closer than your jugular vein be fearing.
Tarrot readings, crystal balls are bait,
For those impermissible things are deceiving.
Fortune telling is humans competing with fate,
In your book of deeds this meeting it will state.
To what is private in your account each,
Is account & opportunity to a better reach.
Fate predetermined written by account,
Unfolding by intent, you know your amount,
The choice to be good exists by guidance,
To follow & emulate to be more righteous.
So don't give up and blame Allah for options,
Since we blame him for all our human notions.
Have Tawakkul and you will in this life succeed,
Since he gave the Prophet and the Qur'an indeed.

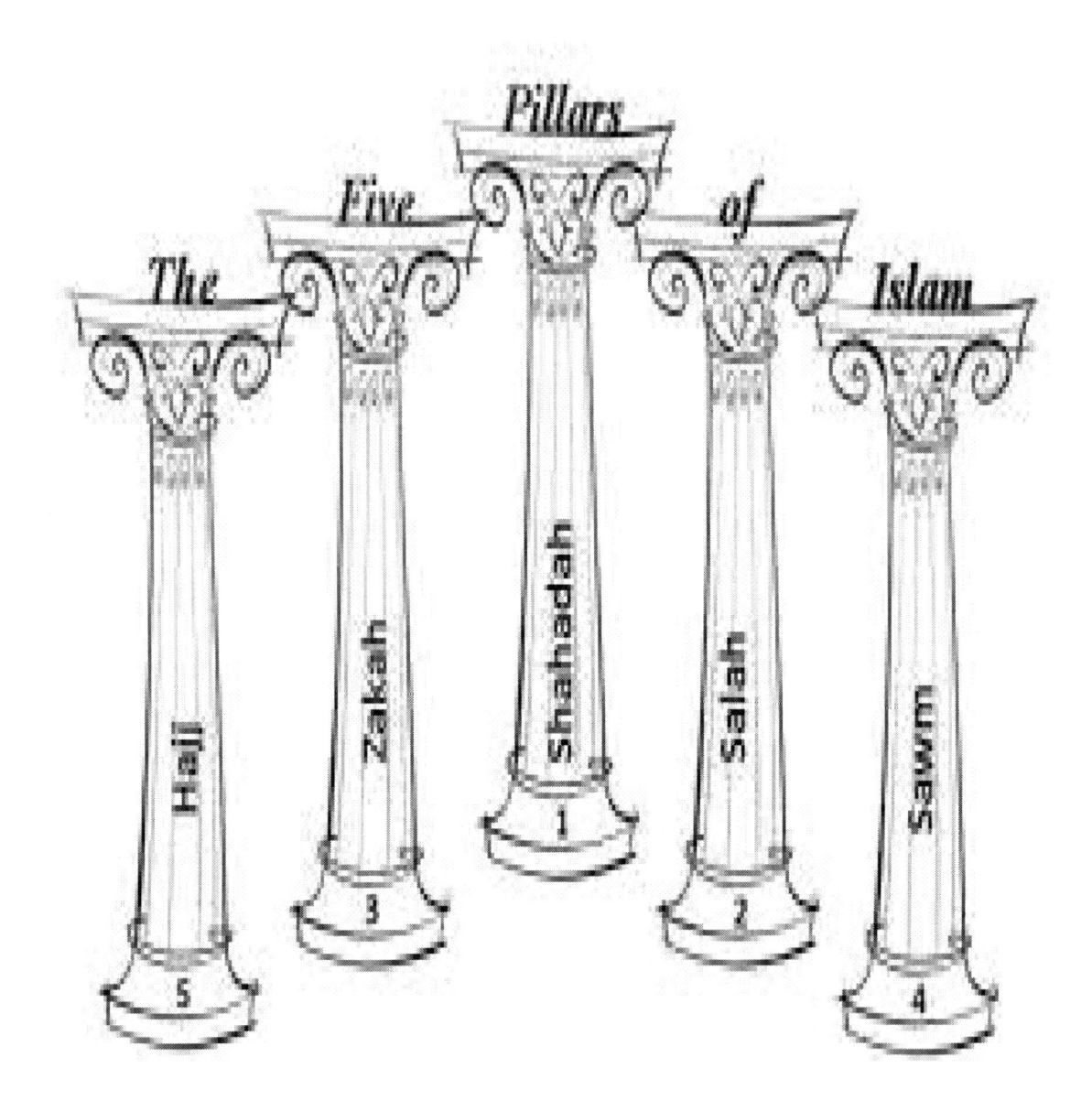

Islam

The Five Pillars of Islam

- 1. Shahadah
- 2. Salah
- 3. Zakah
- 4. Sawm
- 5. Hajj

The Shahadah (Declaration)

The utterance of entry is the testification,
A sincere internal acceptance & outer declaration.
The words are so simple yet comprehensive,
To say them out of mock would be highly offensive.
The Shahadah is the declaration of divine love,
To declare belief in God & His beloved imbued with God above.
The words uttered are to be said with sincerity,
Understanding the nature of belief with complete maturity.
The key part is the affirmation to God,
God as one & the finality of the beloved to Prophethood.
These two declarations suffice in belief,
Since the rest emanate from them without any grief.
God is considered without any equal unique,
Beyond all human capacity unlimited with how we speak.
Other than the glimpses of 99 names et al,
God's majesty & perfection are beyond the mind & all.
Prophethood is deemed to be final & complete,
False ones are considered imposters that compete.
Since finality is confirmed by its readers,
An attesting as with God as one by the true believers.
The Shahadah is for Muslims a simple equation,
An overriding expression of their faith in simple summation.

Salah – The prayer

A time of deep spiritual thought & reflection,
    A unique time to make with God a connection.
Enriched & rejuvenating through bliss,
    A time to raise hands – to everything else a miss.
But to remain firm & God centred,
    As the Prophet of mercy with compassion mentored.
To care about the right way & others,
    Greetings of peace & goodness to sisters & brothers.
East & West there's no competition,
    Except out of goodness their life's true mission.
Less competition but to gain God consciousness,
    With Him is the conversation of the truly piousness.
The prayer is a definer of belief,
    Other than Shahadah it is on yawm ul qiyamah a relief.
Salah is for remembrance & development,
    Self-discipline & with Taqwa complete envelopment.
The prayer is the reading & the request,
    The following & emulation of the Sunnah of the best.
Fajr, Zuhr, Asr, Maghrib, Isha are 5 prayers each day,
    Set times within which Muslims must pray.
Given from God on the night journey Him to obey,
    Sunnah shows the words & utterances for you to say.
Other prayers include Tahajjud & Tarawih in Ramadan,
    Prayer increases Taqwa & the believer's iman.
Other prayers include Istikhara & for the eclipse,
    Those that are compulsory one should not miss.
Muslims are forbidden to pray at sunrise and sunset,
    Worshipping the sun is a sin one must not forget.
The prayer is never a burden on the believing,
    An opportune time to recount the blessings you're receiving.

Zakah - The charity

Charity a blessing to ones wealth,
To share with others to increase their health.
Charity to help those less fortunate,
In circumstances they find often most unfortunate.
Charity ensures humility of the givers,
In comparison to those most grate from the receivers.
Charity increases love & compassion of all,
Remembering those who need it most is your call.
Charity is both obligatory and optional,
To ensure duties are fulfilled – individual conditional.
Charity aids those living lives of hardship,
Slums, shelters, streets, cardboard boxes that make us weep.
To genuinely understand those needs love,
Because God gave us provision to share out of divine love.
Zakah is 2.5% of one's wealth or gold contingent,
Since the law desires kindness and hearts sentiment.
It is based on nisab a set certain amount,
What you give is rewarded in your final account.
It can be given to travellers and to help reverts,
What you give in Allah's way never hurts.
Some of it goes to help those in debt and the collectors,
Also to free Muslims captives from their tormentors.
Zakah is often distributed in Ramadan,
A sign of righteousness and firm iman.
Sadaqah is optional charity in different ways,
It could be an act of goodness & what one says.
Charity aids those truly in need of aid,
It reminds that God is behind the wealth made.
Charity brings love between both sides,
To a world where often the condition of poverty divides.

Sawm - Fasting in Ramadan

Early morning awakenings for Sehri time,
    Food for fulfilment on days from Allah sublime.
Another day of yearning for rewards,
    Remembering poverty & those things one affords.
The month of divine revelation,
    Ramadan with the night of power a time of elevation.
The blessings of the month involve sharing,
    Self-sacrifice from abstaining from food shows caring.
A test of empathy & self-introspection,
    Building between rich & poor mutual connection,
Fasting of behaviours & from food & drink,
    A time of spiritual contemplation to deeply think,
Fasting to aid ones tongue, behaviour & speech,
    To focus on the goals of Jannah they wish to reach.
A long day of patience & striving,
    Remembering those with little or nothing still surviving.
But also celebrating the month of Qur'an,
    A timeout in the year to increase good amal & iman.
Then there is time to make wonderful Iftar its opening,
    No account as they can eat to their fill without accounting.
Some have little whilst others have plenty,
    After a hard day sharing food so no one goes empty.
Some during this month pay obligatory charity,
    Whilst others forgive and avoid any type of enmity.
Then comes time for the prayer of night Tarawih,
    No excuse as satan is locked up the believers enemy.
In the last 10 days is the night of power,
    Some sit the Itikaf in mosque or isolation to seek this hour.
The festival of Eid ul Fitr marks the end,
    To celebrate, reflect and in Ramadan amend.

Ramadan

*R*amadan the joyous and wonderful month
elevated and born from the birth of the Qur'an.

*A*llah the almighty with this month blessed us,
He infinitely does forgive and gives us reasons to live

*M*uhammad (s.a.w.) the Mercy to mankind
received in this month the revelation of light,

*A*ccelerate to the path of spirituality and peace
let the serenity of faith live and release.

*D*ua's are more counted and much accepted
in this time of reward immense at no expense.

*A*ll the Ummah are united by this blessed time
with the Night of power blossoming you like a flower.

*N*o time is rewarded so easy usually to gain us mercy,
showers you like the droplets from the rain.

This month is a connection of people from all places,
united in Dhikr and blessings as equals are all races.

Connections with the poor and those who are meek,
time of reflection on actions and world we speak.

A chance to cleanse and start fresh again,
with this month so many blessings rain.

Preparing on a journey

A deep love of faith shines and lights me in life,
A peaceful path that is protecting me from rife.
Amazing truth really strong and heartily firm,
Tawhid is the only pure monotheism I do confirm.

A unique journey of the Hajj awaits me very soon,
An amazing experience I need, I'm over the moon.
Feelings so deep reside and inexpressible inside,
so grateful to Allah the one on whom I've relied.

Finally I shall traverse on Islam my spiritual way,
Submission to Allah's will, before the Kab'ah I'll pray.
Deep down inside I'm feeling so nervous and scared,
I hope that I travel with strength and be prepared.

I shall apply the clothing of Ihram and its rules,
With my heart and love as the strongest of tools.
I will be in the midst of crowds of Muslims immense,
Equal to all shall I stand with faith as my defence.

Humbled am I and grateful to respond to this call,
As I prepare and comprehend my position so small.
I know this opportunity comes once in a lifetime,
So beautiful and unique a journey to me sublime,

It's simplicity I wish to depart to from worldly greed,
Forgiveness of all is imperatively required to proceed.
Mental and spiritual preparation is also vital to succeed,
So in the name of Allah His praises I will try to read.

Imagined only in thoughts residing within my mind,
Beyond the pictures the reality of Islam I am to find.
Echoes and sounds of God's praises I shall only hear,
This opportunity is a light within my heart very dear.

Hajj

Beauty undefined is the Hajj a spiritual journey of a lifetime of faith complete.
It is the journey that completes our human life that formerly was so obsolete.

        Divine grace falls on those who sojourn on a journey magnificent and unique,
        Utterances of submission do resonate from the world's people rich and meek.

No gathering has ever been seen where the rainbow of humanity shines bright.
It is a journey that fulfils its guests with immense spiritual strength and light.

        Inner peace is found in a place historically the birth of Islam a beautiful deen.
        Its manifestation is shown on its power to modify those who there have been.

The pilgrims declare their journey solely for the sake of Allah and His way.
Never seen in humanity such egalitarianism as they all prostrate and pray.

        Central to Hajj is the Kab'ah which many Muslims will constantly circumambulate.
        It was built by Adam (a.s) as the place to worship Allah and for humans to liberate.

Destroyed it was then during the great flood at the time of Nuh (a.s) in past,
But rebuilt it was by the Prophet Ibrahim (a.s) and Ismail (a.s) to stay steadfast.

        During the Hajj the history of Islam is replayed, coming back to complete life,
        Each believer declares the oneness of Allah and forgets any anguish or strife.

Adam (a.s) landed here with Huwa (r.a) as they were dispelled from heaven,
Tempted were they but sought forgiveness and amended for the layers of seven.

        Prophets and humanity descended from Adam (a.s) who did sincerely remorse,
        What he changed was for all of humanity and the Pilgrims their future course.

Hajra (r.a) the mother of Ismail (a.s) ran desperately in search of water for him,
She was a devote woman who symbolised motherly affection, not human whim.

        As Ismail (a.s) stamped the ground the Zam-zam water emerged as a great miracle,
        His response was overjoyed and calm an example not to be in hardship hysterical.

Ibrahim (a.s) her good spouse was a great Prophet and friend of Allah Most High,
He was told by Allah to sacrifice his son Ismail (a.s) and he devotedly did comply.

        Shaytan tried to tempt Ibrahim (a.s) as Shaytan is the enemy of man and jinn,
        But steadfast and devoted was Ibrahim (a.s) and against temptation did win.

Muhammad (s.a.w) led a great example and purified the Kab'ah from polytheism,
He circled the Kab'ah and enjoined and reminded of Islam, a strong monotheism.

        In commemoration of such sacrifices and purification of the Kab'ah do we pray,
        It's a reminder that people of past were striving so we could walk on Allah's way.

Labayk Allah humma Labuyk, Labayk Allah humma Labayk to succeed,
United collectively as one do we read Talbiyah and nourish our soul its feed.

        Today in huge numbers we arise to take this journey so completely unique,
        Its sublime nature makes it so amazing to describe with words we speak.

May Allah bless us all to journey on this beautiful walk of history today,
May Allah give us the blessing of forgiveness and guide us to its way.

Rejuvenated

My heart was captured on Hajj with a deep sense of peace,
in front of my eyes I saw real human love and faith unleash.
Spiritually fulfilled and covered with my faith Subhanallah,
standing as one in the Saff's in Masjid ul Harem for Salah.

I went on this journey empty and felt spiritually rejuvenated,
finally human souls from the pangs of materialism liberated.
Feeling lonely in previous times and lost in a darkened world,
yet here together united amongst humanity with Islam unfurled.

A sound so beautiful echoed from the minaret with the Adhan,
hearts were brightened and enlightened with strong Iman.
Standing equally shoulder to shoulder as one and side by side,
such compassion for the ummah, a heart with love cried.

Allah has blessed me with this profound and unique way,
a journey like a dream not captured – if only it could stay.
Long awaited, positively amalgamated with times of peace,
Allah granted heavenly happiness's path away from unease.

The Ummah emerged from places like Turkey & the Middle East,
no continental barriers or nationalities hindered to say the least.
Minds and hearts became united singing all of Allah's praises,
happiness extended with smiles elated on all races and faces.

Arafat was a humbling experience and chance to be in faith deep,
all hearts and thoughts poured out in humility as we did weep.
Allah rained down His mercy and gave us a new opportunity,
rejuvenated with Islam and to know that with Allah is our immunity.

Allah's gift and call was respected as we gathered and had left,
reminded were we of those less fortunate with lives that are bereft.
Yet strengthened to persist to stand up for justice and truth,
to traverse back to enhance the lives of old & the Muslim youth.

Ihsan

Ihsan

Ihsan it means excellence or perfection,
Worship of God and developing connection.

"It is to worship God as though He sees you",
How over-empowering, persons it does imbue.

"If you cannot see Him know that He sees you",
Since He is All-Seeing and All-Knowing tis true.

Comes from the word Hasan meaning beauty,
Focuses on your devotion and to God your duty.

Developmentally making beauty happen Ihsan is,
Mentioned in the ayah 90 in Surah on Bees.

It increases your Taqwa and makes you God-fearing,
You know that in your worship He is ever All-Hearing.

It makes you aware that you are in God's Presence,
Acknowledges in you His perfect divine essence.

It is the highest state a believer can be in,
With pure intention and focus you will win.

In worship you focus on purifying your intention,
Constantly aware that God is there within mention.

The purpose of humans is to worship Allah,
This may include it in the form of Zikr or Salah.

It is to worship & believe in God without doubt,
To know there is a greater being with moral clout.

Your finite and you may acknowledge your limitation,
You know to God is glory & clear high elevation.

Humans reflect & have awareness of Allah,
Cognisant of His 99 names such as when in salah.

It reminds the believer from God nought is hidden,
It instils God consciousness so deeply arisen.

Allah

Muslims believe in a strict uncompromising monotheism (mono = one, theism = belief in God). They believe Allah has always been and will always be and that Allah begets not (has no children) and neither was He begotten (born of anyone). They believe Allah is unique and there is no equal or sequel to God. The belief in the Unity of Allah is Tawhid. Allah is the Arabic term for God. Muslims declare the oneness of Allah in the Shahadah mentioned in the aforementioned poem.

Muslims believe Allah has infinite power. Allah has power over us and all that He makes. Allah is over and beyond his creation and hence is Transcendent. Allah has complete knowledge of everything and is closer to us than our jugular vein & hence is Immanent. Allah is Al-Aziz (All Powerful) also known as Omnipotent (All Powerful). Allah is Master of the Day of Judgement. Allah has complete knowledge of everything He is Omniscient (Al-Aleem). In order for something to happen he says 'BE'.

Muslims believe Allah is the Creator. Allah has designed and created each thing uniquely to His plan and has infinite (unlimited) knowledge. Allah has created life, the world, heavens & earth and all it contains. He is the Sustainer & Cherisher of the universe. He created humans and jinn as well as Prophets and angels.

Muslims believe Allah is Al-Rahman & Al-Rahim. Allah's mercy prevails over His wrath. Allah forgives His creation of their mistakes and bestows us with compassion. Allah will forgive & have mercy on any of His servants that will repent. They also believe Allah blessed humans with prophets and messengers to help guide His servants to Jannah.

Muslim beliefs about the attributes of Allah are found in the 99 names in the aforementioned poem. These are names that emanate from the Qur'an the Muslim holy book whose authorship is God who sent the angel Jibrail to reveal it to Muhammad (pbuh).

Alhamdulillah

Allah you have blessed me with the very best in life,
You showed me the only truth and what is right.
You blessed my life with so much beauty and delight,
I thank you my Lord from morning till night.

You sent down to earth so much heavenly grace,
You protected me from wrong & worldly disgrace.
You gave me hope when in life times were rough,
You gave me my life which shows all your love.

Oh Allah how much your blessings I do appreciate,
Your amazing guidance in my life does liberate.
You gave me this smile to express what is deep,
I praise you my Lord so in remembrance I weep.

You gave me many chances after chances to amend,
You gave me hidayah that only you could send.
No one else can encompass so much mercy and power,
Your blessings precipitate on me each minute and hour.

How beautiful and perfect did you make this place,
Nobody else can ever create what you have or replace.
The flowers immense so beautiful they blossom brightly,
So my precious faith in you I hold ever so tightly.

Oh Allah the Merciful you gave me reasons to live,
My mistakes I knew only you'd always forgive,
You gave my soul and this body of mine life to live,
So my heartfelt praise in return is what I do give.

Thank you Allah for your blessings I enjoy always,
Your praise is due all the time without fail always.
Give me much strength to have faith in you so firm,
I know that you're High that every day I confirm.

Allah's blessings

Observe this universe and you'll see the beauty of the moon and sky,
in awe I repeat Subhanallah at the workings of Allah Most High.
My heart does glorify Allah and His guidance it does try to apply.
I question how with such magnificence can we forget Allah and lie.

The universe reminds you of Allah and human weakness and defeat.
The mechanisms of the world let my heart embrace faith and its beat.
We're reminded Allah provides our sustenance each second of the day.
So acknowledge Allah and His beautiful blessings without any delay.

Allah has made such variety with amazing and splendid creations,
Allah also made human diversity as is shown through all nations.
Allah has given us five senses to enjoy such mercies with jubilation,
So we cannot excuse ourselves from our deen and all its obligations.

So collectively sing the song of the bird that flies with open wings,
Rejoice in all the glorious, numerous and superb endowed blessings.
You are fashioned as one of those uniquely existing and gifted designs,
Alhamdulillah, you have been blessed with reason the best of minds.

Allah gave you existence and that itself is manifestation of His power,
He gave you glad tidings and guidance to blossom like a flower.
So please search far and wide for blessed wisdom & knowledge,
Traverse the lands, institutions, universities, schools and college.

So take some time out of your schedule so busy and distracting,
Remember to Allah is all praise and gratitude that's benefiting.
No regret is made and no time is wasted for such act of dignity,
Look deep in your heart and embrace Dhikr and see serenity.

The Prophets

Muslim belief in Prophethood is called Risalah and is one of the articles of faith. Muslims believe that Prophethood is the pure divinely blessed means of communication between Allah and humans. There were 124,000 Prophets altogether. 25 are mentioned in the Qur'an. They are:

Adam	Idris (Enoch)	Nuh (Noah)
Hud (Hud)	Salih	Lut (Lot)
Ibrahim (Abraham)	Ishaq (Isaac)	Ismail (Ishmael)
Yaqub (Jacob)	Yusuf (Joseph)	Ayyub (Job)
Dhul Kifl (Ezekiel)	Shoaib (Jethro)	Musa (Moses)
Harun (Aaron)	Ilyas (Elijah)	Al-Yasa (Elisha)
Dawud (David)	Sulaiman (Solomon)	Yunus (Jonah)
Zakariah (Zecharia)	Yahya (John the Baptist)	Isa (Jesus)
Muhammad (s.a.w)		

Peace be upon them all.

Not all Prophets were messengers as they preached the same message. Only a certain group of them were given revelation which Muslims believe God has the originals within the Preserved Tablet (Lahw al Mahfuz). Angel Jibrail gave the messages from Allah to the Prophets.

Muslims believe a prophet was sent to every nation. But Muhammad (pbuh) was sent to all of humanity. Muslims believe that the previous dispensations (messages) were distorted, altered and changed over time. However, the Qur'an is the untainted word of God and the example of the Prophet has been transmitted by the rightly guided transmissions found in the hadith (sayings of the Prophet) collections.

The stories of the Prophets are called Qisas al Ambiya and are found in the Qur'an with elaborations in the hadith and the Tafsirs (commentary on the Qur'an) of great scholars.

Muslims believe that Muhammad (pbuh) is the final Prophet and he is often called the seal of Prophethood. Muslims believe he is the perfect example that embodied the Qur'an and his example is called the Sunnah which Muslims try to emulate. The message of Islam was completed with him. He is a descendant of Ismail (a.s). Muslims believe he came to fulfil and purify the previous messages that were sent.

In this section I will be looking at a select few of the Prophets mentioned in the Qur'an.

Yaqub (Jacob) (a.s) & Yusuf (Joseph) (a.s)

A prophet was born a blessing of high status indeed,
Born of Prophetic lineage & utmost righteous seed.
Ahl ul Taqwa the best of those through time to lead,
Guided by divine love and message only to help us heed.

He was born with a destiny of continual blessed progeny,
That of Ambiya with blessings from Allah was clear to see.
But tested also by tyrants and their unfair injustice,
With Allah's might the tables had turned for divine justice.

His sons were twelve of whom tribes of twelve were born,
His message to follow the way of good and against wrong warn.
In these tribes others had emanated out of the prayers of good,
As faithful servants since the law of God was to be understood.

His sons were twelve in number a great blessing for him,
Since tribes were they bound to the law not personal whim.
His most loved son was Yusuf (a.s) a pious man divine fearing,
Remembering despite his siblings envy His Lord was All-Seeing.

Thrown by envy and betrayal was he from being loved by his Ab,
Taken by fate to rescue by a passer by the decree of his Rabb.
His brothers throw was covered by false evidence and deceit,
Taken to the father who was doubtful but grieved this feat.

Told from a shirt he was no longer; a story not to believe,
Since destiny would make him greater since envy did deceive.
The well was the place where brotherly bonds had broken,
For the other brothers to gain favour through this act olden.

The father was a man who was truly in this saliheen,
Firm on his tawakkul and his way on the righteous deen.
How upsetting it was that he had even lost his sight,
To be brought back through Shifa from Mujiza of his sons light.

The son was employed as a house servant to his master,
On an outing he was tested so his response had to be faster.
He was accused of actions he would never ever have done,
But the wife of the master had ill conceited intent on the Prophetic son.

She was caught on her plan to make him in this intent look sinister,
Sent to the court of the King and the deciphering of this disaster.
He was placed by others of her court who hurt themselves at his sight,
A man of taqwa his handsomeness was born of divine blessing & light.

A new place was yet made for him as he was unfairly sent to Jail,
His encounters gave him the chance to prove the decision was a fail.
A set of questions from dreams were postulated to him for reading,
His knowledge was divinely blessed so his reading was for heeding.

The dream interpretation became an analysis of what would befall,
But what would be recovered after this time of loss and fall.
His understanding was appreciated by the one who did ask,
So he was allowed to work again in a higher position for a new task.

From a fate that seemed at the well to have ended at that time,
Had resulted in a prosecution for an innocence free of an alleged crime,
Though destiny had for his fate regained freedom and a new position,
From his loss to what he would eventually regain on his life's mission.

The rest of the sons were asked to get food for his house's need,
The father was not happy to send Benyamin (r.a) to this act or deed.
Since in his trust with his other sons he lost his favourite child,
Like a lamb to the slaughter of ending to a cover up I remind.

He sent his sons and wanted a promise he would not be lost,
A dual risk of loss of his house would be a reminiscent cost.
But fate would have him left there to the dual in latter no zero,
Left with the righteous whom he loved a story of the fated hero.

His brothers came with intent to gain for their house and fill,
It was a request given that they were to complete and fulfil.
The sons arrived to make a purchase and take leave after a meeting,
Little did they know that they had given their envied brother a greeting.

The brother thrown in the well out of envy was the decider,
In their bags a chalice was placed a test of truth the finder.
They denied its theft left in Benyamin (r.a) bag as evidence,
Taken in as a prisoner for a past that required repentance.

Their bags were empty as far as they knew with the brothers loss,
They went with dual loss of brothers and ungiven goods.
When they reached home they saw their bags were filled,
Only part of the task thus was completed and fulfilled.

The father was told of what had happened and became distraught,
As with the past his son was a trust his comeback he sought.
He remained hopeful that his sons now missing would be found,
Since his taqwa and knowledge gave him tawakul, he was firmly abound.

Whilst Yusuf (a.s) and Benyamin (r.a) established truth about the past,
That he remained alive despite the sight of him at the well last.
Both brothers were no longer prisoners but became truly aware,
Of fatherly love, historic envy and the tests that remained there.

He sent them back as requested each through a different door,
He was in shock and dismay that his son had been called a choor.
When they came back he explained to them eventually all truth,
A wrong committed to him by actions that were portrayed as brute.

The son out of mercy said you have all of the past been forgiven,
From envy against fathers most loved; ill deeds and intent were driven.
He then gave a garment of shifa for his father's sight to be restored again,
From blindness to sight his father's happiness came from missing pain.

When he saw his son happiness overwhelmed at him being alive,
Fate saw them come together in his midst where they did arrive.
A progeny was to be born with great tests from this given place,
The closure to slavery, tumult and the unjust Pharaonic disgrace.

But they lived happy for much time with a high place in the court,
Where the truth he together with them had eventually sought.
The father was not taken seriously upon knowing he would be alive,
How much he yearned despite the tumult inside his desire would thrive.

Upon the mistakes of his brothers he said they were forgiven,
Since by envy in this situation they had wrongly been driven.
He had an enemy satan who desired for this division and friction,
As he stated for his reason thus to forgive from his opponents addiction.

The story is one born out of the miracles of life given as a trust,
In this situation taking care with righteous rearing is a dutiful must.
The test is to take children from this world to the path to win,
To guide them uprightly and guard them from desire to sin.

Endeavouring to fulfil agreements and maintain good is required,
Since the Prophets wished to be right with God as was divinely desired.
Hence the quality of Taqwa that brought blessings was admired,
From this path one must work hard with strength and not be tired.

Yusuf (a.s) was a man envied though he was a man of success,
Yaqub (a.s) was righteous and his dua answered as Allah does bless.
The sons were all undoubtedly in a trial and evident test,
But the pious and God-fearing like Yusuf (a.s) win and achieve the best.

Musa (a.s)

Listen to the story of Egypt once upon a time,
Innocence was taken and Pharaoh perpetrated a great crime.
The Hebrews were taken to be his slaves night and day,
Pharaoh believed for them there was no other viable way.

He ordered for all the Hebrew newborn to be killed and slain,
He had no consideration of their misery and pain.
But Musa's (a.s) mother was not going to heed Pharaoh's call,
She protected her family & to injustice she stood tall.

As Pharaoh roared to kill innocence in one go,
Musa (a.s) was placed in a basket and in the river Nile flow.
His loving sister had ran to see where her brother would end,
He went in the house of the enemy Pharaoh – no Hebrew's friend.

Taken by Assiya (r.a) she was tender and sweet,
Little did Musa (a.s) know it was his fate he would meet.
Sheltered by the man who called himself God and more,
It was Musa (a.s) identity challenged for him to explore.

As he grew in Pharaoh's house, the world he finally understood,
Reminded was he of his roots and the protection of motherhood.
He ran away from the house he no longer accepted,
He came back and affirmed Allah and Pharaoh he rejected.

Allah spoke to him from a burning bush to his awe,
He knew then on what his role and purpose was for.
Allah gave him the staff to help let the Hebrews free,
But it was a challenge for Pharaoh he never thought would be.

Musa (a.s) became a great Messenger and Prophet,
He ventured for justice and knew money couldn't buy it.
Allah helped him to deliver from Egypt his nation,
They were to be freed from a life of injustice & aberration

Allah sent great punishments as a sign for Pharaoh and Egypt,
But ignorance subdued him as from the truth he slept.
But losses were his, realised as he soon also wept.
Allah freed the Hebrews and Musa's (a.s) promise was kept.

Musa (a.s) was called to Mount Sinai where Allah spoke to him,
Meanwhile his people worshipped wrongly the golden calf and did sin.
But God out of His infinite mercy forgave them of their crime,
But human amnesia shows they make the same mistake each time.

Musa (a.s) left the Torah and his uprightness as his legacy,
He showed bravery in the face of tumult, tyranny and the enemy.
Firm with faith and a manifestation of God's power was he,
May we all benefit from his example that forever shall be.

Maryam (a.s) & Isa (a.s)

As a little child so small you came into a world as a stranger,
Little did you know from birth onwards you were in danger.
With your mother's love she held you ever so close and so tight,
Allah had blessed her with you in her womb and so much light.

Maryam (a.s) prayed and prostrated for many periods ever so long,
She had dedicated herself to her Lord and didn't do the wrong
As the angel Gabriel came – she was given the glad tidings,
She strived in her time for truth for that was enlightening.

Righteous and blessed with faith and a Prophet as child,
She saw and embraced her child and for him smiled.
She was promised paradise as the best woman of all time,
Her loving nature and unconditional faith was sublime.

Amazingly she carried her child when others had doubt,
She trusted Allah who gave her protection and helped her out.
She beautifully symbolised the love between mother and offspring,
Her memory and uprightness will always remain living.

Dedicated to the temple for remembrance of Allah was she,
She was an example to us all of righteousness indeed.
Her son the blessed Prophet Isa (a.s) brought truth,
He confirmed the message of all Prophets such as Lut (a.s).

She was shocked to conceive without any bond with man,
But Allah said 'Be' and can just do whatever He can.
Like Adam (a.s) & Huwa (r.a) were the first of creation,
Yet without conception humanity descends with many a nation.

Isa (a.s) did not die, he ascended to heaven from the cross,
God protected him, it was the betrayer and enemies loss.
He miraculously had spoken whilst he was in the cradle,
Kind & considerate he helped those in need & less able.

From critiques his veracity was doubted by the wrong,
Nevertheless him & his mother still stayed strong.
Like Adam (a.s) He was born miraculously with no dad,
He was confronting justly the people who to him were sad.

He by God aided others by healing the blind & the leper,
Isa (a.s) had brought the dead back to life, the helper.
He breathed life into clay to form amazingly a bird,
He had spoken righteously & conveyed Allah's word.

Isa (a.s) was taken to be killed, but was raised to Allah in heaven,
The layers of which there are for various types of people seven.
Al-Mai'dah is entitled after Isa (a.s) disciples' heavenly feast,
He received God's bounties & never gave up in hardship the least.

His life on earth includes when he will come to fight the Dajjal the liar,
He will come to defend the faith and save us from the smouldering fire.
He will guard against him and finally slay the Anti-Christ in one go,
To him is success and goodness; a divine lover the believer's amigo.

From the white Mosque in Damascus he will emerge before the end of days,
He will rectify, amend and help us in our wrong doing ways.
He will live and deal with the exploitation and unbelief in our world,
His call will resonate far and wide and won't go unheard.

May Allah bless us to acknowledge both Maryam (a.s) and Isa (a.s) who were great,
And send them our prayers and let us emulate them as it's never late.
Both symbolised total dedication, compassion and were always striving,
It's these qualities we need to embed which are required in the Akhira for surviving.

Muhammad (p.b.u.h) A mercy to mankind

In Mecca 570 CE born was a shining light,
    A man of wisdom, the truth & foresight.
His mother died whilst he was small,
    Born to her the greatest Prophet of them all.
From Tribe Quraish of family Banu Hashim,
    An illuminating light he was and living dream.
The divine call at 40 in cave Hira he received,
    From Jibrail the angel who had believed.
Given the final revelation of the Qur'an,
    A living miracle from Allah for jinn & insan.
Born in an age of shirk & ignorance,
    His message was the greatest deliverance.
At a time when people practiced idolatry,
    He received divine revelation in solitary.
He already believed that Allah is One,
    This light of Tawhid in Arabia further shone.
Allah could never be idol or divided,
    The truth was the proof the reality decided.
The message had spread far and vast,
    Of the final Prophet people had learnt fast.

In a darkness so many people had fell,
    Far from heaven on the destructive path of hell.
Tyranny & tumult were daily norm,
    Money and power would bring much form.
But to this situation a Prophet arose,
    Muhammad (saw) the one Allah (s.w.t) chose.
His message for some came as shock,
    He worked strenuously around the clock.
To spread the given divine revelation,
    For us to succeed with true emancipation.
Preceded by the story related in Surah al-Fil.
    Born a descendant of the Prophet Ismail (a.s),
At 6 He lost Amina (r.a) his mother,
    Father before he came, wet nursed by another.
Born to nobility he lived in humility,
    A man of the greatest faith & sincerity.
Taken care of by loved ones at the crib,
    Incl. granddad Abdul Mutalib & Uncle Abu Talib.
He was taught the great trade routes,
    Familiar was he of the evils of greedy brutes.

During the time women were treated ill,
        The thugs and brigands would get a thrill.
Many girls were unfortunately buried alive,
        Lucky were they who would often survive.
Slavery and injustice was common place,
        As was judgement based upon class & race.
Many good people they would disgrace,
        Only their own kind they would embrace.
People would often gamble and drink,
        In ignorance & delusion they would all sink.
People immersed themselves in wrong,
        The weak were oppressed by the strong.
Vendettas seemed to be common and rife,
        Innocent people were often facing strife.
They worshipped gods of their making,
        Though the truth they were all forsaking.
Religion was being sold at an easy price,
        Apparent was the immorality & the vice.
Humanity was being bought and sold,
        Mind-sets were hardened & deeply cold.

In Makkah he had first preached,
        Limited by the leaders to few it had reached.
He taught them about monotheism,
        Since indulgent was practice of polytheism.
He conveyed the messages of past,
        With completion as he was of Prophets Last.
Central was One God the affirmation,
        To live with morality with true confirmation.
He was a great Prophet with a vision,
        Though initially met with jeers & derision.
This was of justice the miscarriage,
        But at 25 support was offered by marriage.
A great businesswoman did ask,
        Who was supportive of his Prophetic task.
He accepted and she was very good,
        A first convert & pillar that understood.
She sent him to a Christian monk,
        To him the recognition of prophecy sunk.
The evidence was manifest & clear,
        To Allah (S.W.T) blessed was this man dear.

Persecuted he left for Madinah,
    To songs of Tala ul baduru alayna.
In Madinah he set up a constitution,
    A leader he was and man of revolution.
He united factions and warring tribes,
    Building success with truth not bribes.
The faithful community grew and grew,
    Many members to this light quickly drew.
The ansars took in the muhajireen,
    Muslims as one for the sake of the deen.
In his mosque Bilal (r.a) read the 1st adhan,
    The call for prayer for the people of Iman.
He fought the battles of Badr & Uhud,
    Not out of choice in face of zulm he stood.
Eventually they went back to Makkah,
    Purifying it from idolatry for dhikr of Allah.
What he brought could not be replaced,
    Injustice and wrong he rightly effaced.
He was a revolutionary in many ways,
    A man worthy of much accolade and praise.

The early Muslims had begun as a few,
    With time the masses grew and had grew.
They would gather at Dar al Arqam,
    Increased had they with their pious maqam.
Khadijah (r.a) was the Prophets wife,
    She was truly a good blessing in his life.
A business woman who was widowed,
    With the rhythm of Islam with love flowed.
She assured the Prophet of his greatness,
    She gained for herself the heavenly status.
Summaya (r.a) was of Islam's first shaheed,
    Killed by the merchants power and greed.
Aisha (r.a) was his last wife a scholar,
    Knowledge, intellect & a great preacher.
Hafsa (r.a) was entrusted with Qur'an,
    That was safeguarded with her firm iman.
The early women were very proactive,
    Of one another they were truly protective.
They were very pious & well learnt,
    It was a place in heaven they had earned.

The prophet's companions were loyal,
      Inheritors of the thrones of heaven royal.
Fatima (r.a) was his beloved daughter,
      In marriage Ali (r.a) his cousin sought her.
Parents of great children of Jannah,
      Loyal followers of the Qur'an & the Sunnah.
Ali (r.a) had fought with a dual sword,
      Defender of Islam & servant of the Lord.
Hasan (r.a) & Husayn (r.a) were loved,
      The grand children of God's most beloved.
Abu Bakr (r.a) was known as As-Sadiq,
      Truthful & good with wisdom he'd speak.
Umar (r.a) began as a early opponent,
      Embraced Islam & became its proponent.
Bilal (r.a) was 1st shackled living in slavery,
      But recognised was he for faith & bravery.
Zaid (r.a) memorised the Holy Qur'an,
      A righteous servant imbued with his Iman.
Hamza (r.a) uncle of the Prophet (s.a.w),
      The message he truly had understood it.

Prophet gave the great Khutbut-ul Hajja speech,
      The farewell sermon that we often teach.
It was a really heart rendering speech,
      One that to all of humanity would reach.
The equality of humanity of all races,
      The love of Allah and His countless graces.
He taught to care for all and women,
      To remain steadfast and refrain from sin.
On the night of Al-Miraj was a great sign,
      ascended to the 7 heavens to the divine.
On al Buraq he miraculously firmly rode,
      Reaching the unseen heavenly abode.
He spoke to the great prophets & Allah,
      Given the divine command of enjoining salah.
He led all the Prophets in Al-Aqsa mosque,
      What a mighty and blessed miraculous task.
Affirming completeness of Prophethood,
      Was a man upright, humble and perfectly good.
Reaching a state and stages we never could,
      Incomprehensible how he is misunderstood.

He illuminated hearts and minds,
       Perfection in him one always finds.
With a smile people he would greet,
       He never stopped his work ever upbeat.
He was trustworthy the al-amin,
       A man of peace & keeping the earth green.
He never gave up but always strived,
       In the face of tyranny his faith survived.
He was a perfect example to lead,
       Person of generosity not entrenching greed.
He was patient and one of servitude,
       Perfect mannerisms & not abrupt or rude.
He cared for young, old and the weak,
       With intelligence & articulation he'd speak.
He enjoined good and forbade wrong,
       His faith was firmly solid and strong.
He removed the shackles of slavery,
       Fought in the face of injustice with bravery.
By example he led to the right way,
       To Allah only with conviction he would pray.

To difficulty he gave perfect solutions,
       Ridding us of addictive pollutions.
Love, aspiration and motivations he gave,
       Blessing from Allah the Prophet, the brave.
A great Prophet the others he affirmed,
       The truth completed & now confirmed.
His companions stood by his side,
       His teachings in life they would abide.
He left a vault of thinkers and leaders,
       A strengthening community of believers.
Who struggled early from persecution,
       A community of the mightiest revolution.
Blessed with his example & the Qur'an,
       Were the Sahaba and mumineen of Iman.
To him instantly true believers will always bind.
       He cared, for all his life showed he was kind,
He was undoubtedly a mercy to mankind,
       A man of love, dignity and an intelligent mind.
Though to the past we cannot rewind,
       Living is the light of the mercy to mankind.

His teachings had covered all of life,
        The path to remove misery and strife.
The path to Jannah to us he gave,
        Endowed with mercy he always forgave.
He showed the way of purification,
        For body and heart to gain full elevation.
He emphasised on true modesty,
        Humility, faith and to have lives of piety.
He warned of the test of wealth,
        A trust from Allah as is ones health.
A balance required to avert all fights,
        He taught responsibilities and rights.
His determination kept him going,
        With firm Taqwa in Allah the All-Knowing.
In his way there was no slowing,
        Acceleration as the truth was growing.
Success & prophethood his kingdom,
        He gave us knowledge and wisdom.
He was an embodiment of Qur'an,
        A Prophet built with the light of Iman.

More fragrant and beautiful than a rose,
        At home he helped delouse his clothes.
He would cook & clean in the home,
        Led life simple not like an emperor of Rome.
He was loving, caring and very kind,
        In him love & compassion one does find.
He was radiant & would smile,
        Concerned with the inner not outer style.
Humble he did not raise himself up,
        With his wife Aisha (r.a) shared the same cup.
The welfare of others for he cared,
        His possessions with others he had shared.
He stood up for people's rights,
        Prayed & prostrated for countless nights.
His concerns were the next world,
        Where all our deeds will then be unfurled.
Many will automatically love him,
        The mercy to humanity not personal whim.
He left the message final & complete,
        Remembrance of Allah with every heartbeat.

The Prophet taught treat your women well,
      He warned of impending punishments of hell.
He taught that piety was most required,
      He expressed it in the Khutba al Hajjja admired.
It didn't matter if your Arab or not, black or white,
      It was your level of taqwa that had to be right.
He warned of the signs of the day of judgement,
      With hadiths his teachings the Qur'an supplement.
His warnings show a deep know of eschatology,
      Of increase like behaviour against normal biology.
He warned of signs only uttered by a Prophet,
      He taught us to all be mindful and not forget.
He warned of evils to come like the beast,
      The rising of the sun from the west than east.
He warned of the anti-christ known as ad-Dajjal,
      He guided his ummah from the liar's dark amal.
Many of the minor signs have already come,
      Our salvation is in following his way to become.
He was a warner and warned in advance,
      How blessed were those who saw his glance.

He enlightened us to the second coming of Jesus (a.s),
      A Prophet who with the Gospel did teach us.
He held in high esteem Ibrahim (a.s) the Wali Allah,
      He taught to send him salutations in Salah.
He taught like Musa (a.s) the importance of law,
      In Rasulullah you find uswutun husna & no flaw.
He led all the Prophets in prayer at al-aqsa Mosque,
      He ascended to Heaven on Isra wal Miraj a night task.
Honoured he was the final of all the Prophets,
      His life and deeds acclaim respect and merits.
Like Dawud (a.s) & Sulaiman (a.s) he was wise,
      With his teachings and life you see & realize.
He established that divine justice was the way,
      He taught us to strive in the path of Allah all day.
Blessed was he & angels send him salutations,
      A blessing descended on earth for all nations.
A guide that shone radiantly with true light,
      May we strive in his way with strength and might.
The Seal of Prophets he was the final one,
      Many hearts and respect had he already won.

Born in the Arabian Peninsula was he,
    To liberate us with truth & set us free.
He faced persecution, tribulations & test,
    His fine example proved that he was best.
In short it was a very difficult start,
    But illuminated was the Prophet's heart.
A man with wisdom truly smart,
    Who taught us about divine love as art.
He warned us of the signs of the end,
    Precautions and the path to truly amend.
He made clear ilm of eschatology,
    Warnings of using magic and astrology.
Upon Allah he would truly depend,
    The wrong to the right he would mend.
He was of Prophethood the end,
    A gift and great blessing a true God send.
Salutations upon him we send all,
    The one who guided us to the divine call.
Salutations upon him we should all send,
    As do the angels upon Allah's chosen friend.

The prophet taught us compassion & love,
    With mercies delivered from high above.
His message was truly empowering,
    Filled with mercy and blessings showering.
No-one was left behind or neglected,
    The message instantaneously elevated.
He will intercede for the believers,
    A message of success and peace he delivers.
He was the greatest man of all time,
    An example outstanding and truly sublime.
He was a great Prophet & teacher,
    A fine visionary leader & excellent preacher.
With all the Prophets he was connected,
    Blessed Prophets, angels & by Allah respected.
Salutations & accolades he deserves,
    As of heaven & closeness to Allah his reserves.
He was sent as a mercy to all mankind,
    Mission accomplished in his life you find.
A man of beauty in heart, body and mind,
    Blessed Mustapha Muhammad (s.a.w) the kind.

"Verily, Allah and His angels shower blessings on the Prophet. O Believers! Bless him and salute him with a worthy salutation." (Qur'an 33:56)

Blessed Prophet

Blessed Prophet the great role model & Messenger of Allah,
Upon whom blessings are sent to in every daily Salah.

You're status is very high and your close to our heart,
You led a life humble and you're intellectually smart.
Your example as one of perfection supersedes all of time,
Your name and life were blessed by Allah the divine.

You helped people to intelligently reflect on reasons to live for,
For all our mistakes, problems and tribulations you gave a cure.
You always had uncompromising faith in Allah to succeed,
Your life was simple not worldly and free of the pangs of greed.

You saved us from the claws of injustice, oppression and hate,
You taught us the path of guidance with truth & love of faith.
Oh Prophet of Allah your truly unique and one of the kind,
Your honesty, purity & intelligence blessed darkened mankind.

Your life for the ummah is elevated and esteemed as the perfect guide,
You are undoubtedly the one who is the Al-Amin as you never lied.
When times were filled with despair and tumult you always tried,
You had strengthened the ummah to stay strong and not to divide.

You are the mercy to mankind, Muhammad Mustapha (s.a.w).
To our hearts your extremely dear and near, never far.
May Allah help us to emulate the life of the best of mankind,
And guide us to the truth to see the light of Islam and not be blind.

Blessed Prophet the great role model & Messenger of Allah,
You shine brighter than all the worlds' diamonds or any star.

Muhammad (p.b.u.h) – A mercy to mankind 2

Born in Mecca was a gift and shining light,
Blessing to humanity guider to the right.
The final Prophet sent to all of mankind,
Blessed by the divine his body and mind.

Blessed was the path that he would walk,
Only with words of righteousness he'd talk.
He was soft and tender, sweet and gentle,
Words of compassion quite sentimental.

He is the final Prophet & of intercession,
After whom there will be no succession.
A mercy to humanity sent for all of time,
Radiant like the sunshine truly sublime.

A beautiful example total and complete,
No tyranny or falsehood could defeat.
Liberator of humanity from shackles of slavery,
Stood up for truth to oppressors with bravery.

He cared for the poor, orphans and weak,
Eloquently & intellectually he would speak.
He taught by example and led to the right way,
With divine revelation & guidance he would pray.

The angel Jibrail gave him from Allah the Qur'an,
He taught him the way of Islam, Iman and Ihsan.
Aisha (r.a) described him as the walking Qur'an,
Filled with spiritual light and the nur of iman.

His Sunnah is a model to the path of success,
Illuminating as the light of creation the best.
His legacy to this truth itself will truly attest,
Holding all the keys to success on life's test.

He was known as Al-Amin trusted and kind,
In his life humility & perfection you do find.
He taught us to turn to Allah who forgives,
Complementing the perfect exemplary way lives.

Islam's path to success

Islam derives from the Arabic word salam which means peace. It is the submission to the will of Allah. It is a religion of over 1 billion people spanning countries, cultures, races and continents. Its followers are called Muslim which means those who submit to Allah. It is centred in belief in One God called Allah and the belief in the finality of Muhammad (pbuh) as the Messenger of Allah.

The path to success is found in the implementation of the Qur'an and Sunnah as helped by the scholarly elite who have codified the law and faith derived from these two primary sources. To succeed in this path you have to search for knowledge as it is a compulsory duty on the believer. Knowledge enhances the believer and helps them discern right from wrong. There are scholars and teachers who are practitioners of the faith that teach and illuminate to the path of success through knowledge and inspiration as effective role models who emulate the best role model Muhammad (pbuh).

Islam

Islam has the truth that every human can believe.
Islam has such strength to give us firm belief.

Islam is the radiant soul that lets the body live.
Islam is the spirit that teaches us to forgive.

Islam is the ideal to guide us on our path.
Islam is relief from earning God's wrath.

Islam is a force that brings humans together.
Islam is an energy whose power goes on forever.

Islam is a light that shines in our lives so bright.
Islam is the reason to go on each day & night.

Islam is the sanctuary for all those rich & poor.
Islam is the incentive to succeed – it is the open door.

Islam is the happiness that increases everyone's smile.
Islam is the answer to all those doubters in denial.

Islam is the key that unlocks the mysteries of the world.
Islam is the soothing rhythm that resonates beyond word.

Consumption with the love of faith

Faith, I have become so consumed with your taste and essence,
You bring me inner peace as you present me with your presence.
You show me yourself in so many ways you strike me with awe,
You give me positive vibes when all see in me so many a flaw.

Faith you help me the sojourner so loyal to my life's real quest,
You give me motivation and compassion to affirm with true zest.
You give me company in loneliness as a friend in life's short test,
You are the incentive for me to be encompassed with the best.

Consumed am I the believer like Divine Lovers of the past,
like them I have a shining light of love which will always last.
You're my friend and my conscience to heed the divine call fast,
You protect me from the smouldering fire which makes me aghast.

Faith your joy travels around my body like the pumping of the heart,
Your little recipe of happiness is viable to all those truly smart.
You give me blessings that my heart protects like a precious treasure,
You're irreplaceable with any type of material goods or other measure.

Faith embrace me in your company and let me feel your loving breath,
The one that keeps me going in my life from the pangs of human death.
Faith manifest yourself in my empty life when I'm feeling lonely,
Give me immense spiritual renewal and love as it's what I need only.

Faith shower me with your mercy and kindness happiness and joy,
Make me amongst those loved with words that deserve no ploy.
Be my guide, my friend, my search and my spirit of heart,
Ya Rabb guide me along life's journey in fulfilment from the start.

The Teachers

Great scholars and masters left their legacy,
From the blessings they had from Allah's mercy.

They need not be present as their legacy lives on,
They have with them victory as they have won.

They gave us wisdom and knowledge good,
radiance & light so the truth we understood.

Flowing with emancipating words & intelligence,
With the keys to unlock the maps of evidence.

Sleepless night & days often they had spent,
To unravel mysteries of truth and what it meant.

Great leaders and thinkers gave us ilm the gift,
For us to ponder, think, reflect & stay aright.

They devoted their time each & every day,
To guide the seekers of truth to the right way.

Lips thirsty hungering for the truth fulfilled,
Hearts humbled and truth in them instilled.

On the path of seeking truth they all started,
After Its acquiescence its legacy they imparted.

They never wrote just by pen but also by heart,
They mastered wisdom and faith the greatest art.

Words were not merely ever said just of token,
Accountability present on the finite words spoken.

They taught not only to follow the faith & its creed,
But to conquer the ego & do good in every deed.

Thank the teachers whose legacy shines bright,
They are to a darkened room an illuminating light.

The teachers had the greatest teacher to guide,
Muallim the Prophet with Allah on their side.

Champions

Looking for a new champion or hero,
Everyone's been struck by numeral zero.
Looking for the right defenders,
A test of who will amend us.
Looking for a champion to lead the way,
Inspiration & heroism in what they say.
Looking for articulation & fine speech,
Someone who can lead & someone who can teach.
Looking for someone to save the day,
Genuine intentions - not covetousness for pay.
Looking for someone to stand very firm,
To be clear so likewise the rest can affirm.
Looking for someone who aims to succeed,
For vision & success for others not personal greed.
Looking for someone with speed & ambition,
A champion for all to attain a lofty position.
Looking for someone who genuinely cares,
Does not fear the game of opposites & dares.
Looking for someone who knows the needs,
To defend & protect innocence with their needs.
Looking for a story of success in the making,
The clocks are ticking – it's time for a champion
the world is waiting!!!

The greatest champions were the messengers. However Prophethood is complete. The new champions include the scholars who are the deemed inheritors of Prophets and those that lead through dedication and inspiration and have the traits of the poem.

The Right Path

Live a life covered with love not hate,
seek a life blessed with Taqwa & the true faith.
Yearn for Allah's mercy and not His wrath,
follow deen al-Islam it's the spiritual true path.

Don't sell your iman to any worldly desire,
work for jannah the path guarding from the hell-fire.
Remember this life is short and will expire,
so don't be deluded form the truth to be admired.

Sometimes you treat life just like a game,
you dream of immense wealth and lots of fame.
But happiness lies in something much more great,
embrace and be covered with the faith to liberate.

In life were tempted to go astray and be sinning,
but you've got to be strong and join those winning.
This life is full of many temporary testing pleasures,
don't be deluded by such fake and false treasures.

Trust Allah completely and let your soul be empowered,
seek the divine blessings and with mercy be showered.
Allah's guidance will fulfil us and make us complete,
take the path to success not the dunya so obsolete.

Recognise with everything else there is defeat,
but iman is serenity, success and eternally sweet.
It is the protection from an everlasting heat,
let dhikr of Allah be your every heart beat.

Subhnalahi wa bi hamdihi

The faith most dear

More precious than rubies, diamonds & jewels,
Is the faith and all of its life changing tools.
Beauty is its good steps and guidance with it rules.

The faith has its heavenly doors open to you all,
Embraced by its good words and its divine call,
Seeds of successfulness within you it does install.

Islam the blessed complete faith from the divine,
With a unique gift of the Qur'an the living sign.
It's withstanding the test of time is truly sublime.

The Qur'an is the miracle sent from Allah above,
A guide complimented with the Sunnah to gov.
Sent to guide humanity with the Creators love.

In the faith you find help of every matter & kind,
As it exhorts you to think and use your mind.
In this you find yourself clearly logically defined.

It is the best route to submit to and truly follow,
It fills inside what was formerly void and hollow.
Spiritually strengthens from any wound or sorrow.

Deep Thinking

The journey of life is truly quite amazing from the time preceding birth, birth and the life itself.

The magnitude of such grandiose blessings is certainly worthy of awe, acknowledgement, gratitude and praise to its prime source that is Allah.

The Islamic faith espouses a beautiful and strict uncompromising monotheism. This attestation to the oneness of Allah is known as Tawhid. It is a belief that encompasses every aspect of a Muslims life and worldview. Importantly it sets the foundation for understanding the connection between Allah and humans.
Tawhid is expressed through the basic utterance of the Shahadah. – the words of the declaration of faith that embraces people to the fold of Islam. The Shahadah is:

'There is no god except Allah and Muhammad is His messenger.'

A Muslim not only declares their belief in Allah, but explicitly rejects anyone else as God or any equation with Allah of any kind. The elevation and uniqueness of Allah is then naturally apparent.

The Islamic faith sets the foundational basis for human existence in the centrality of the source of their origin, i.e. Allah. This rationalises human existence with a sense of focus, purpose and direction as espoused of their creator. As a consequence humanity are shown like sojourners on a spiritual quest of life – to reach favour and gain the pleasure of Allah to whom they subordinate their life for gain.

Allah's existence is not challenged or denied, but complimented by the Qur'an and its exhorting of the believer to reflect on its signs 'ayahs' which manifest their one true Creator Allah.

The belief in Allah has been the source of discussion, debate, antagonism and faith for diverging groups of people. Humans have long found themselves immersed in philosophical debates through time on the nature and existence of Allah. Science has also been used, exploited and referred to in this process. However, with or without debate humans are made to confront the question of their existence – are they here by chance, do they exist as a random product or are they beyond a body? Such questions have continued through time.

Islam has dealt with many of these questions and offers itself as the light in the passage of darkness. Some of these arguments have been dealt with by the likes of Al Ghazali and other great thinkers.

Imam Abu Hanifa who has a whole school of thought named after him eloquently deals with this through a simple, humoured and rational piece. Abdur Raheem Green in a talk on God explained his argument as follows:

"...We found one of the early Muslim scholars when he was challenged by the atheists to prove to us that God exists...made an agreement with them he said let me meet you after the sunset prayer at the side of such and such river at such and such time. And they were waiting for the scholar, the atheists. They were waiting and they were waiting. And after some time, a long time he still hadn't shown up. So eventually when he came they were chastising him and were saying "why were you so late and what happened to you?" this and that. And he said, "You know the most amazing thing happened to me. I got to the

river and I couldn't find any way to cross. So I was walking there, walking up and walking down and thinking how am I going to cross the river. These people are waiting for me. And what am I going to do so I sat down scratching my beard whatever. And thinking how am I going to get across. Suddenly the tree fell down in front of me and divided itself into planks and out of the ground popped nails. And this boat start forming itself In front of my eyes. So I got in the boat and the boat carried me outside the river and that's how I got here." So they said… "Come on you don't expect us to believe such nonsense. What rubbish is this?" He said "but why not? You ask me to believe something even more incredible that the heavens and the earth and all it contains is a product of chance and coincidence"…".

One essential set of arguments that deals with the question of the existence of God is underpinned on the premise of design. The argument maintains that the existence of design in the universe would allude to the fact that there must be a designer behind it. Just as common items we utilise and find point by their structure, design and mechanisms to their designer and manufacturer. The complex nature of the world and all it encompasses must also point to a designer that is greater and beyond the design and is the ultimate designer of all. The ultimate designer with infinite qualities is none other than Allah. This argument is articulated through the continual references to the signs 'Ayah' of Allah mentioned in the Qur'an. The Qur'an does not allow the believer to just accept faith but exhorts the believer to use their divine gift of critical faculty to reflect and ponder the wonders of Allah's creation and power of design. The intricacies of even the spider and bee and their abilities is pointed to.

The Muslim jurist who is also renowned for having a school of thought named after him, Al Shafi also beautifully tackles the question by reference to design. As follows:

The famous jurist, Ash-Shaafi`, was asked: "What is the proof for the existence of God?"

He replied

"The leaf of the mulberry tree. It's colour, smell, taste and everything about it seem one and the same to you. But a caterpillar eats it and it comes out as fine silken thread. A bee feeds on it and comes out honey. A sheep eats it and it comes out as dung. Gazelles chew on it and it congeals producing the fragrance of musk.

"Who has made all these different things come from the same type of leaf?"'

(Islam The Natural Way, Abdul Wahid Hamid, Mels 1989, p,5)

The question is quite perennial – who is the source of these designs and processes at work? The answer is self-evidently Allah whose names manifest His ever presence and importance in and beyond the universe. The above example is only one. They very study of biology rests on the design and processes of so many things within and around us. Whilst the study of science can explain how these processes function and relate to each other, alone it cannot rest without an ultimate answer to the inception and source of all such magnificence. The designs cannot come out of nothing – they are the product of much intelligence, thought, design and power which must come from a supreme designer, a designer unlike all the designs whose magnificence is unparalleled and cannot be equated as the source of their making throughout time. The designer is none other than Allah who as the very concept of Tawhid demonstrates cannot be equated or matched to anything else.

Jalalauddin Rumi the spiritual master renowned for his work Mathnawi also tackles in beautiful and rational form the questions related to God's existence. In his unique writing style he exhorts his readers to reflect on deep and salient questions that allow us to reach the evident conclusion on the existence of Allah. One of the questions he postulates is:

> **'The unbeliever argues: 'I can perceive nothing apart from what my sense perceive.' But the unbeliever never reflects that the perceptions of the senses give news of that which is beyond their perception; they pick up hints of hidden wisdom. Indeed the purpose of the five senses is to indicate the individual to seek this hidden wisdom.'**
> **(Rumi: Mathnawi, IV 2878-80)**

This beautifully demonstrates the fact that the divinely gifted abilities humans have been endowed with point to things beyond their reach, one of which is hidden wisdom. This hidden wisdom through the utility of the senses has been the reason for great human endeavours, accomplishments and achievements throughout time. Were the faculties only used and seen as limited objects, then we would not have half the advancements that we benefit from.

The other questions he postulates are:

> **'Those who deny God often say: 'If the spirit of God were present in Nature, we would be able to see it.' But if a child cannot see the intellect within an adult, does that mean the intellect does not exist? If a rational person is insensitive to the movements of love, does that mean that love is an illusion?'**
>
> **(Rumi: Mathnawi, III 4796-7)**

Both arguments rest on the fact that on the one hand we have scope and ability to do much beyond what we deem ourselves capable. Additionally, as well is the idea that these abilities exist for us to ponder and reflect and search for the hidden wisdom. But at the same time we recognise the finite nature of humans, their limited ability and the fact that there are things greater and beyond what the eyes see which should make us ponder the greatness of what lies beyond us. That greatness which leaves its mark and from which we emerge is none other than Allah.

The aforementioned scholars were wise and erudite. Muslims through history have given birth to great sages whose hearts speak when the pen draws ink to paper. Who inspire and guide intellectually the youth and the old on a variety of issues. The scholars in the Islamic faith are considered to be the inheritors of the Prophets. Divine wisdom and immense knowledge has flowed through many through time with some elect who have had Karamat (miracles). These stand testimony to their piety and God consciousness. This cognisance of God brings to them the fruits of miracles, success and leaving behind legacies. Though the legacy of Prophets is greater and their miracles manifold called Mujiza. The Prophets, Messengers, Scholars and sages were all deep thinkers.

Allah's existence

Allah The Great is and always will be for all eternity,
Though an atheist would postulate this couldn't ever be.
It is denial compounded in ignorance that causes such rejection,
But with the proofs I will give there won't be any objection.

Existence cannot emerge from the inception of nothing at all,
Because each thing has a cause no matter how big or small.
The universe could not just form itself from a big explosion,
Otherwise this world would not be orderly, instead full of erosion.

Human intellect and the power of the mind require intelligence,
Failure to recognise this uniqueness would be sheer nonsense.
How could the complex nature of the human body just be?
Or even the order of the universe and how from a seed comes a tree.

If we are here for the survival of the fittest – why's this the case?
Why are we to work hard as death would be the last phase?
But human virtue and rational suggest purpose and design.
They point to intelligence and complexity, naturally to the divine.

If nothing has an ultimate cause then why do we all live?
It is capitalism that is promoted here, not the virtue to give.
How do the planets orbit and animals exist and function here?
Something greater would allow them to work in motion and gear.

If God did not exist then who has complete power over all?
Are you suggesting that death is cessation and life rolls like a ball?
Then why do we have feelings so deep within and roles so high?
Why do animals follow their own course and like birds just fly?

God has given countless signs in the Holy Qur'an – the guide,
It is filled with truth and withstands the test of time as it's applied.
It exhorts the unbeliever to challenge its writ if they have the truth,
It sets moral and intellectual guidelines and bears rational fruit.

If science has so much truth they claim God is not needed today,
But why is there so much fallacy and theories that change each day?
What exists is the subjectivity and the limitation of human kind,
It tells you what goes on but from ultimate truth remains blind.

God's existence is necessity as its power permeates our limitation,
It baffles me how out of two we have now so many a nation.
We exist in a world which is undoubtedly so complex and unique,
Blessed with five senses with which we see, smell, hear, and speak.

Could we really just be the product of chance and random cause?
But then why so much order in the face of chaos? – have a pause.
If suffering is the excuse for denial – have you solved it with death as cessation?
faith speaks about life as a test and moral behaviour is required – a better explanation.

So accommodation and acceptance of God should not be hard for you,
It is the solution to your life, your purpose and is rationally true.

My perfect world

My perfect world created, why is your beauty still unheard?
You but shine with me the rainbows and life's every word.
You're filled with so many pleasures, challenges and delight,
I wake each day with your sun's rays empowering so bright.

Beautiful world your very intricacy is mind baffling, God's call,
You're filled with variety undeniably immense great and small.
You could not be here illogically just by random chance or play,
Your everything amazes me to how it runs its own unique way.

Unique are all the inhabitants you completely seem to cater for,
Just when a discovery ended, there's always room for more.
Science is limited with human worldly capacity so ever brief,
You're blessed with things that attest and give internal belief.

Why do all the philosophers and scientists pride in their discoveries?
Were it not for the beauty of the world they would all cease.
Complex are the designs of the one so perfect unlike any other,
who created us from something small, and placed us in our mother.

If Allah Almighty did not allow for perfection would you be here?
But take a cursory glance and Allah's presence is always near.
No person of power or prestige can create and account for the world,
So belief in God should resonate and not go ignorantly unheard.

So easily people point to tragedy and pain as the end of design,
But this can't serve as a denial to the world's origin from the divine.
How the world floats in the galaxy just amazes most and me,
So open your heart to the truth and in Allah you will believe.

Questions

On the journey of life so many questions,
With alternative views and suggestions.
There is always the need for reflections,
Building in life your spiritual connections.

The traveller seeks to find the right road,
Trying to attain the heavenly abode.
Dealing with tests & the usual load,
Need to be focused with the correct mode.

The traveller stops and really ponders,
On all of Allah's countless wonders:
It is the truth that you wish to gain,
A life free from misery and pain.

Questions start to arise like those below
so that you may seek & also know:
Have you ever wondered of the beauty
of the stars and the night sky?
Have you ever wondered at the fixation
of mountains & the birds that fly?
Have you ever thought about how
the world has really come about?
It's complex mechanisms point to a
supreme designer there is no real doubt?
Have you ever wondered at the
complexity of the body & human mind?
If science and humans were divine –
why are they still on a daily find?
Have you ever thought about the life
in the sky and the life in the sea?
How you all exist, not from ex-nihilo
but Allah's command 'BE'

Humanity recall such wisdom, complexity, uniqueness is from Allah the wise.
Open even your rational faculties, how can you then not realise.
Alhamdulillah, Mashallah, Subhanallah

Inspiration

What inspired humans to build the finest architecture,
What inspired the bees to produce the finest pure honey?
What inspired the birds to hum sweet tunes in the morning?
What inspired the great calligraphers and artists to paint & draw?
What inspired the spiders to build the most intricate of webs?
What inspired the greatest oratory through time?
What inspired the wonderful gardens & parks arrangements?
What inspired the greatest marvels of the world?
What inspired the silk worm to produce silk?
What inspired the waterfall to flow beautifully?
What inspired light and water for the formation of a rainbow?

What inspires one may not inspire the other, but the inspiration & drive behind them can be a positive driving force to move forward. In most cases one would point out to the inspirer of inspirers, Allah the Creator of creation and the giver of intellects through his divine wisdom.

To be inspired….my faith inspires…Allah inspires

The Rose – the majesty of the garden

The rose & its design make one truly think.
Its colours vary beyond red, yellow & pink,

Amazed was I by the sight of a beautiful rose,
In its bright lit petals all its glimmer arose.

From a small little seed into a delight it grows,
Above the others from the love God bestows.

By roses in gardens one sees this lovely sight,
Grown with love & the food of water & light.

The rose covered with beautiful colours bright,
In to branches with petals & thorns of might.

Designed it is immaculately by God that knows,
Abounding this small gift and blessing the rose.

Praise Allah who gave this grandeur to the rose.
Who created variety & beauty in what He chose.

Miraculous stars

Stars in the night sky,

truly in awe they mystify.

Shining upon us light,

In the darkness of night.

So far away yet close,

Beautiful like a rose.

Colour from high above,

A blessing from God's love.

To the eyes ever a delight,

as they shine upon us bright.

They amaze sense & sight,

To the eye they're a delight

A compliment to the moon,

They have their own tune.

A message of hope, light,

& a prayer for a future bright.

The child & the Sages - reflective help from the Wise

A child in need once asked for help as required,
However, the child was uncertain of the outcomes they desired.
So trust was essential to ensure that no problems would arise,
The child thus trusted the decisions of the wise.
The child asked questions from complex thought to those with knowledge,
Insufficient were the limitations from acquisition from school to college.

The child's postulations included the question of being,
The wise reflected on theology, science, on Allah the All-Seeing.
Their response explored the dimensions of creativity and design around,
The laws of nature & complex matters that we know to be sound.
They said the world was created and designed by Allah Al-Khaliq,
Everything has existent knowledge from Al-Aleem & Al-Malik.
These knowledges like DNA come from God whose names are superior,
To suggest they're from nothing to common sense is clearly inferior.
It is clear nobody has attributes like the 99 names of God,
Signs and manifestations around us; to say otherwise is odd.

The child thus asked the question of how to deal with pain around you,
A conflict in discussion arose on whether it's natural or moral evil though.
They stated the need to tackle & challenge it in ways you could,
By lawful ways since it was something you should.
Humans have freewill to make choices and are to account for Moral evil,
It occurs when Allah's laws are disobeyed for his opponent the Devil.
Natural evil is a sign of the power of Allah manifest and a test,
In times of such crisis others responses bring out in humans the best.
Another issue they decided to task on was the issue of purpose,
Since it would expand on the rights & wrongs causing pain without or with purpose.
The way to deal with something causing hurt and grief untold,
Was given extensive responses to effects & causes that would unfold.
The way to deal with pain is to heal and aid the wounds of hurt,
By protective, respective & collective measures to ensure no further spurt.

The question next postulated was in regards to achieving,
There was a unanimity that it required amongst them believing.
Some of it was self-belief & goals to achieve the needs,
Some of it was to ensure they left a future by planting seeds.
Seeds beyond the ones of literality to those of mark of good for others,
To share what's right & leave what's good for fellow human sisters and brothers.
To follow the laws that were given for them to be morally guarded,
To remain steadfast with hope even if they were weak hearted.
The way to achieve was to fully exert themselves through learning,
To ensure lawful hard work would result in success & good earning.

The child then asked the salient question of why people become ill,
The wise reflected & pointed to the aforementioned as some of God's will.
Though some is affliction not just a test & some are victims of cruelty,
Many innocents often suffer from mock and brutality.
All illness except death though may be treated,
It's with strength & immunity internal & external to beat it.
Not beat as in hurt further since it may not heal,
But to give a lawful prognosis and not a harsh deal.

The child then moved to the question of death and its trial,
A difficult question for most but its discussion is worthwhile.
The wise contended as with your surroundings you will perish,
So make the most out of life & hold the good you cherish.
Close to the heart since at any point death may appear,
Not an experience to stumble though humans compete with God out of no fear.
The wise stated that their lives were like timelines with inception & end.
That all one day will be taken to grave or above,
That God brought you into this world out of His love.
The ground that they walk on may be their resting place,
To gain as many good deeds to be imbued with divine grace.
The experience may be easy or very painful to circumstance,
Once God takes you, there won't be any other chance.
Though it may be taken unfairly by injustice,
Murderers & malicious intent be warned it belongs to God so don't touch this.
It may not remain one piece of body contingent on what it has endured,
But on the day of reckoning it will be re-formed as one as though it is cured.

The child then asked the question why do we grow old,
The wise laughed & commented life through stages will unfold.
From existence to soul, to birth, infancy, junior until senior,
Some may be taken much earlier by God the superior.

The child then asked why innocents were taken unfairly often,
The wise contended by stating that is the test from hospital to coffin.
That God takes those slain for God to a heavenly abode,
Including innocent babies & mothers dying giving birth - heavens owed.
Where they rejoice with pleasures & luxuries of those most deserving,
Remain steadfast & in the face of tribulation totally unnerving.
Remember your accountability is to Allah (SWT) the one worthy of serving,
So that you gain the best out of life remain totally unswerving to wronging.

The child then moved to the question of why we were made in different races,
Unique to God each fingerprint from His love He made you all with differing faces.
The colours he made you brought vibrancy & richness to you all,
To respect & understand diversity as God's gift was a divine call.
Some of you He made with differing complexions in differing places,
Abounding you all with His countless blessings and graces.
Not to look in the mirror & feel in any shape inferior,

Know that inside you all share the same type of interior.
He made the world diverse equally with many colourful creatures,
He left you with revelation to guide you by the good intentions of teachers.
To inspire your lives He made you many colours as with the world,
So everything would work consistently together in harmony as in God's word.

The child then asked the question what is the key to wars,
So many are often fought with casualties it must be a negative force.
The wise contended that it is their least preferred domain,
One of death, destruction & in many cases a huge amount of pain,
The wise argued that in all places people felt a need to protect,
But only the greedy tyrants would hurt innocence out of disrespect.
The wise then stated that sometimes there are needs to intervene,
Ideally with peace the preferred way by God to keep everything humane.
Wars have two sides and in some cases more than that,
Sometimes over justice or personal gain an unfortunate fact.
Sometimes they all forget that life is a sacred gift,
Taking it from the earth or humans is a dangerous shift.
Preserving and taking care of things precious is vital to all,
Peace can stop carnage or war in its dangerous way take us to a fall.
Ideally the wise stated that peace & negotiation was important,
Certain things were pivotal for all since were connected globally resultant.

The child then asked about the question of poverty in countries,
Was it the doing of God or greedy human enemies?
The question was at times Theodicy if not otherwise deep,
There were people in the world that lacked shelter and places to sleep.
Some poverty was unfortunately the cause of war the aforementioned,
Under false & unjust sanctions impediments to life were often sanctioned.
Those decisions reaped ramifications including illness death & impediment,
The situation of poverty & the conditions is no game or experiment.
In so far it's a serious issue to those who often endure it,
It may be game play & experiment to the unjust that deprive every bit.
Furthermore, it may only essentially be a God given test,
For the rest of us to lawfully share God's gifts such as food as the best.
The circumstances of poverty may vary from person to person day to day,
It may be finances, war, violence, tyranny or even what they privately say.
Not all poor may consider their situations in the same way,
Some poverties are physical but their riches may be faith as when they pray.
This reinvigoration has no stoppage since it gives internal content,
That some of us are envied whilst others are unfortunate to circumstances sent.
Though poverty may be a trial for those who feel its heat,
The wise contend count your internal cells and being as millions like every heartbeat.
If the natural blessings are all taken with gratitude,
With charity & love we can increase in the aid of others with servitude.

The child then asked the next questions of the nature of the world's existence,
The sages did not tire back to history. Theology & much more they reminiscence.
Theories of science were often posed as fact,
Though speculation on changing research the details aren't exact.

The theories of the world were not the same as that of humanity,
Scientists contended the big bang for the world & evolution to others an insanity.
Premised on observation & the hypothetico deductive methodology,
Varying thinkers reach multiple conclusions based on faith or science even biology.
The world could not exist out of nothingness since it had a beginning,
The complex nature of the world required a designer to be winning.
Winning an existence of complex structures & designs that co-ordinate,
Even in nature & the self we find complexities innate.
The world was made by God the Creator mentioned by God so atheism is over,
Requiring a complex thought to the designed mechanisms like the world by a Creator.
The layers & structures in the world & their constant flow & balance,
Are to most suggestive of a world detailed by a maker & not by chance.
Had the world not been designed it would have lacked cohesion,
Breakage & inconsistency would not be the way to existence – it would lead to destruction.

The child then asked what is the proof of things beyond,
It was an impending question that others could not completely respond.
Beliefs certainly varied from person to person on things other that exist,
A question the sages felt the fools would avoid, misconstrue or resist.
The outsider would contend their figments of their imagination,
That the images of things beyond are only mere nothingness of hallucination.
The wise made clear the infinite God & finite humans weren't the same,
That in the hands of money makers some things are nothing but a game.
That sight & sense & what's around required thought and reflection,
That the magicians in the world would have such other show of illusion.
The tricks & games of the sorcerers & illusionists were of another kind,
As opposed to the Lord of the worlds the Creator of many beings & humankind.
He created Jinn and Angels not every eye can see,
He commands and creates with the simple word 'Be'.
Some things are definable & visible to all human sight,
Some things were beyond us like stars amidst the beautiful moonlit night.
Non-reachable & non-visible are things below & above to normal vision,
But in those who believe in God there are things in His know not requiring derision.
What is visible to some may be out of their understanding,
Things beyond can't be rejected because it's more commanding.

The child felt the wise gave sufficient responses to the questions,
It meant the wise thinkers had helped with the best responses & suggestions.
The child after reflecting & much more pondering intelligently surrendering,
Reached deep reflection & faith from what the wise responses were comprehending.
The wise were thanked whilst sill derided and jested at by the fools,
The sages had only good intent to the travellers and their tools.

To be humble, to learn & earn lawfully with right,
With this your success through iman will result in heavenly height.
Acknowledge Allah and His revelation authority and supreme law,
Then the world & all issues will make sense free from finite flaw.

Ameen

Irreplaceable

Irreplaceable every life Allah has created,
Irreplaceable every Prophet Allah elevated.
Irreplaceable every second you have ever lived,
Irreplaceable the Qur'an that you believed.
Irreplaceable the truth my Lord preserves,
Irreplaceable all the unique DNA cells & nerves.
Irreplaceable all the unique identities Allah made,
Irreplaceable the logic of all the things Allah forbade.
Irreplaceable the miracles & blessings of motherhood,
Irreplaceable the lives of innocence often stolen,
Irreplaceable the heavenly award for deeds golden.
Irreplaceable the holiest of places for rejoicing,
Irreplaceable the concerns Prophets were voicing.
Irreplaceable the enveloping petals & design of the rose,
Irreplaceable & unique the God of all the above who knows.

God vs Satan

Once upon a time a spirit came to fruition through fire,
He refused to obey Allah & hence became the head of his desire.
His desire was of his failure to accept others on the right way,
As servants of God even if Adam (a.s) was made of clay.
He was told to obey the command to bow down to Adam (a.s),
A man on the righteous path of the deen of Islam.
Though he was himself tested by the rivalrous foe,
Satan refused & from then on the way of discontent he'd sow.
God gave him the option to be humble,
But he considered his matter higher so he did stumble.
They decided not to have a continuum so they parted,
Satan lost the best – to abyss he departed.

Adam (a.s) was tested in the heavenly garden by him,
The deceitful liar intended his failure for his own whim.
He was told with his wife not to eat from a tree forbidden,
However Satan whisperings misled as his intent was hidden.
Resultantly they lost their place in the heavenly garden,
But with position on earth their faith was firmly harden.
But Huwa (r.a) his beloved wife went with him to earth,
From the inception of humanity their first birth.
No rival to the One, who gave them a position,
To lead lives of righteousness on this oath to Godly vision.
The foe himself became agitated, angered & lost,
He decided with his helpers to ruin the good at any cost.
His internal need became to argue & cause many a rift,
He focused on wrongdoing when obedience to God was the gift.
The gift to open respectfully with good intent,
To safeguard throughout life with grateful sentiment.

God Most High the one with the most beautiful names,
Always wins over the competitor & his deceitful games.
The victory within this is to those who aim for goodliness,
In this life your faith is to be spiritually fulfilled for mightiness.
If Satan claims a victory through his game & play,
His victims will account in God's court here on Judgement day.
So long as one strives with firmness & conviction,
They'll win over Satan's desire for evil his prime addiction.
He promotes sins like alcohol, riba and drug taking,
Conflict, violence, greed, theft and human trafficking.
He may offer against you & the faithful an errand or advocate,
He may offer you sins fruited with temptation his witch-hunt.
But the naïve may be subdued to his whims and ways of delusion,

I reach my thoughts as at the very inception,
God has won in truth, inception, summation & conclusion.

The Sky

Look & see high above you the amazing sky,
As made by God whose above His creation high.
In it you see the birds fly upwards towards the sky,
Without any resting place up there we can't deny.
The sky comes as an amazing noticeable blue & white,
Comes with countless colours & changes day & night.
The sky with an amalgam of wondrous clouds of rain,
Keeping the earths vegetation ready for human gain.
Nature & humans also benefit from this downpour,
Something much longed in scorching heat – the sore.
Whilst, not everyone appreciates the sky & its rages,
Nevertheless, God's miracles came from it through ages.
The sky we know an amazing wonder to put you in awe,
A unique canopy and shelter from the sun you saw.

Women in Islam

Whoever said that in Islam woman has no role to play, or is of no significance other than someone who knows nothing of the heritage of Islam, which has had women in its centre in almost every field. The modern Muslim woman is told that her Islam is one of oppression and she must leave it if she is to taste the benefits of the free world for the new woman whose first name is liberation. However such portrayals fail to recognise the roles of prominence that the women of Islam have had in shaping its very being and heritage for centuries meanwhile the rest of the world was continuous in its exploitation of women. Injustices women face in the world such as violence, forced marriage, ill-treatment and sexual abuse are all the volte-face of the Islamic faith, the Prophetic example and the way.

In Islam four women have been elevated with heavenly status and reward for their uprightness, conviction, modesty, God consciousness and piety.

The four women who are promised paradise:

Anas ibn Malik (r.a) said: 'The Prophet (p.b.u.h) said:
'Reckon with the outstanding women of all nations: Mary (a.s), and Khadija (r.a), and Assiya (r.a) the daughter of Muzahim, and Fatima (r.a) the daughter of Muhammad (SA.W).'
(Tirmidhi and Dhahabi).

Aisha (r.a): <u>The scholar of great talents</u>

- She was the daughter of Abu Bakr (r.a) and a beloved wife of Muhammad (p.b.u.h)
- ¼ of the legal traditions of Islam come from her
- During the Caliphates of Abu Bakr (r.a), Umar (r.a), Uthman (r.a) she gave legal advice
- She related 2210 sayings of the Prophet (p.b.u.h)
- She transmitted to at least 77 men and 8 women
- She had knowledge of medicine
- She was a mathematician – gave advice on inheritance
- She was a fine poet and had good knowledge of history
- She was a commentator of Qur'an

Ibn ata a well respected scholar said of Aisha (R.A):
'A'isha was among all the people, the one who had the most knowledge of fiqh, the one who was the most educated, and compared to those who surrounded her, the one whose judgement was the best.' (Ibn Hajar, al-Isaba)'

Khadija (r.a):
<u>The independent, faithful business woman and faithful wife</u>

- She was a wealthy business woman
- She employed the Prophet Muhammad (p.b.u.h) and was so impressed with his character that she sent someone to ask for his hand in marriage to her

- ❖ When the Prophet (p.b.u.h) was given the first revelation, he went to her straight after when he was in shock and she comforted him and gave him her support and reassurances
- ❖ She was the first to accept the message from him
- ❖ She was a pillar of support for him through thick and thin.

Maryam (r.a): <u>A woman of purity</u>

- ❖ Her mother Hanna (r.a) prayed for a child to dedicate to worship Allah in the Temple, when Maryam (a.s) was born she was dedicated to the temple. This was usually for males only.
- ❖ She is the head woman of the women in Paradise and the Prophet (p.b.u.h) said of her: "Khadija (r.a) was preferred over the women of my community [umma] as Maryam (r.a) was preferred over the women of all nations.'
  - ❖ (Tabari, Jami, 111, 264).
- ❖ She was a modest and devout woman who was born of a blessed womb and whose womb was blessed with the miraculous virgin birth of Jesus (p.b.u.h). Both were to suffer the hardships from their society. Yet both were made as a sign to all the nations.
- ❖ She is favoured and honoured. In her devoutness and sincerity in hardship and grief shines her radiance and her success.

Fatima (r.a) <u>The humble and pious</u>

- ❖ She was the daughter of Khadija (r.a) and Muhammad (p.b.u.h).
- ❖ She was an upright God-fearing servant.
- ❖ She was the blessed mother of Hasan (r.a) and Hussain (r.a) the two loved grandchildren of the Prophet who will be the leaders of the youth in heaven. She was the wife of Ali (r.a)
- ❖ When the Prophet was ill he told her he was not going to recover from his ill health and then upon her reaction he told her the next secret she would join him next and then she laughed.
- ❖ She firmly stood by the side of the Prophet through hardship and ease.
- ❖ She is honoured from the womb she emanated from and her womb from which emanated the Prophets loved grandchildren.

<u>Other great women of Islam</u>

1. Sumayya (r.a) - the first martyr of Islam
2. Hafsa (r.a) – the daughter of Umar (r.a) who was entrusted to keep safe the first collection of the Qur'an. Here is a woman trusted with the words of Allah, Alhamdulillah!
3. Assiya (r.a) – the wife of Pharaoh who challenged & rebelled against his treatment of people and self-worship, the woman who took Moses (pbuh) in from his basket and convinced Pharaoh to keep him!
4. The great mothers and daughters through time who were truthful, righteous and follow and followed the path of the Prophets making daily sacrifices for Islam.

Women are not insignificant in Islam; they have shaped Islam and the course of humanity. Without women, there would not have been great men; together they make the best team. Women in Islam have been and still are:
1. Assertive
2. Independent
3. Thinkers/shapers of the world
4. Business women/Doctors/Poets/Work In all good careers
5. Great Mothers
6. Women of faith and Prosperity

Hijab

The Hijab has in recent times become synonymous with an oppressed, deprived, uneducated and burdened burqa clad woman, neither civility, nor liberty are her attributes, or the type her undemocratic and freedom hating patriarchal society wish for her thus. The religion of Islam simply becomes one of men's rights and women's responsibilities. However, Islam needs to be portrayed and viewed on its on terms which are far more beautiful, spiritual and enhancing.

Many of us who observe the Hijab do it out of choice and conviction. Out of divine love this attire is worn that has stayed in fashion through time for the purpose of modesty.

The Hijab does not form or serve as a hindrance to the intellectual development of a woman, but the societal conditions she finds herself in. It is amazing how so many hijabis are dismissed when applying for jobs, because they freely choose to dress modestly. This is a sheer injustice and cannot be tolerated. Where is the freedom loving society now? Where is the society that judges on merit and quality and recognizes the full potential of women? I hear the silence and so do you. This society becomes no different from its 'fanatical' counterpart. The difference is meanwhile our Muslim counterparts do not make extravagant claims of 'liberty, equality, and fraternity' we do.

As ideals we have models that are as thin as the plastic manikins outside the shop windows, a society where plastic surgery is rife and identity crisis is almost never ending, as is depression, does not suggest freedom or liberty.

Islam brings to this challenge a simple yet beautiful concept, that of modesty. Indeed the interpretations of Hijab differ amongst Muslims - but the consensus remains balanced. Indeed, the Muslim world needs to wake up, and give its women the opportunities Islam blesses them with. Our history is full of well respected, educated, women who are very exemplary. From Eve (r.a), Mariam (a.s), Khadijah (r.a), Aisha (r.a), and the many female scholars and pious women in our history, resides our success and heritage. These are women who are emblems of modesty, faith, sincerity and success, and the greatest success of the believer is with Allah, and this is where we should aim. It is common though for people to speak about the abuses of Hijab by some of its wearers, but just as a bad doctor should not be our reason to devalue medicine, or a bad lecturer to devalue education, so likewise those who abuse Hijab should not be an example of the Hijab or to a wider plane Islam. We have better examples, and it is those whom we should seek.

It has been said to me by friends that they cannot see the reason for wearing Hijab because of the weakness of men. But the Hijab is a commandment and if one cannot wear the Hijab, than why does one pray or fast in Ramadan? Only because it is an Islamic injunction that Allah (S.W.T) has prescribed. Why do we keep our jewellery and valuables in a safe place, so as to safeguard them and because of the weakness of a criminal to commit a crime. Likewise, beauty is a valuable or a trust from Allah (S.W.T), and this trust is to be preserved via the Hijab to safeguard you from the immodest. By wearing the Hijab you do not become the best Muslim, arrogance is not an attribute of a believer. However, the garments of modesty supersede the garments of human designers as the garments of modesty are from the one that designed humans, fashioned them and creator of humans and is closer to humans than their jugular vein. He is closer to us then our own selves and knows His creation best and what dress is best, worn by women through time. Faith and actions are intrinsically linked. A good heart is shown through good action, as good action is shown with a good heart. The action of wearing Hijab is of this category.

Women of Success

In Islam we encompass a plurality of great women of success,
Emblems of piety and righteousness are they of the best.

Great women surpass the time of which preceded us today,
These women worked in various spheres and yet bowed down to pray.

We begin with our mother Huwa (r.a) the wife of the first man,
Of her do we descend as part of Allah's great plan.

Assiya (r.a) the assertive wife, who questioned Firaun,
It was justice, humility and taqwah for which she is known.

The mother of Musa (a.s) protected her Prophetic child,
She was reunited with her son by Allah's permission and smiled.

Maryam (a.s) a faithful servant of Allah stood out within her time,
She was blessed with Isa (a.s) without being touched or any crime.

Khadija (r.a) was not only a business woman but a widowed mother,
Her sincerity stood out and she received the Prophet in marriage and no other.

Fatima (r.a) exemplified a woman of great tenacity, who always strived,
Her simplicity and strong conviction in Allah always survived.

Aisha (r.a) was a great intellectual of disciplines and woman of thought,
Her knowledge was to her unique and could never be brought.

The Qur'an was entrusted in the chest of Hafsa (r.a) for safe keeping,
She was dutiful and the Qur'an resonated in many spiritual hearts beating.

These great women were not of a calibre so small or insignificant in need,
Their contribution to women and civilisation is driven by love, not greed.

It is under the feet of the mother that Paradise does lie – hence her high esteem,
Her high standing is like a beautiful light emerging from a small beam.

Without the role of women there would certainly be no great men now,
So women in Islam are important and with their examples we are endowed.

May Allah help us to regain the liberation that Islam has given to its women,
May Allah bless us to lead upright lives away from lives of sin.

The Veil

No threat is my countenance that sees beyond the cloth I wear,
Yet passers-by are amazed and shocked and give a frozen glare.

But free am I in my veil from dress codes so disclosing of the body,
It is the internal values that should be valued to recognise somebody.

The media often capture images of my sisters with negative captions,
This results in Islamophobia and intolerant unwarranted reactions.

I am not the woman of a silent garment as it speaks a million words,
My hijab is my wings with which I open and fly with freedom's birds.

My hijab does not restrict me to household chores and the tune of man,
Liberated am I the spiritual woman that can do as much as they can.

My garment symbolises not how good I am but more so my identity,
Don't be clouded by those who try to exploit it – they're hijab's enemy.

The dress code was given as a blessing from Allah to guard modesty,
So dress clearly isn't about exploitation but protection as you can see.

A garment often ridiculed as absent from modern design and outdated,
But it's not in the eyes of humans but God I wish to be highly rated.

If my dress encroaches my liberty and impedes a worldly progression,
I speak my mind and have a career like any other is my suggestion.

I am not closed to the world but tentatively aware, intelligent and acute,
That my path is based on justice and standing in the face of those brute.

My dress is a veil not of mind and treachery compounded with deception,
It is a reminder to me of purity and modesty the best path of redemption.

Next time you see me do not be afraid for the cover is only a light to see,
I am imperfect but sincerely strive and its deep inside that you will find me.

The dress is so often captioned and headlined as a simple depressing veil,
But it is my boat on the universe of spiritual quest with which I do sail.

Hijab

A dress code of faith & for those God Fearing,
Garment of righteousness & those true believing.
Hijab is for modesty and humility as your seeing,
A statement through history and time still keeping.

If rubies, diamonds, & precious gems are protected,
The same & better for the precious woman is expected.
Covering and keeping away from the glances rejected,
Guarding and honouring dignity of the emancipated.

Shouldn't be frowned and mocked by those hating.
No need to be misguided with the wrong imitating.
Covering is not an impediment but truly liberating,
A reminder of Allah and Spiritually emancipating.

Modesty is a good, righteous, and spiritual stand.
Throughout history and the world one can still scan,
Modesty is not relegated to woman but also to man.
Found in Abrahamic traditions through times span.

The Hijab is of behaviour and not just the dressed,
Through guarding modesty and gaze it's expressed.
Never is its wearer impeded or in life regressed,
Because the identity and concept is by God blessed.

Adhering to the divine injunction is for all a duty,
It reminds that we should be judged on inner beauty.
Not to be denigrated and seen as others booty.
But to be proud of identity and fulfilling a duty.

It does not make one perfect & is not to be abused.
It is not shackling but beautifully flowing and loosed.
Regardless if the ignorant are insulting and bemused,
The God consciousness to wrong aren't ever amused.

It does not make one insignificant for not being loud,
Better to be unique then to follow the wrong crowd.
Inner strength and outer affirmation will help you win,
Guarding you from committing wrong action and sin.

Upon people it's a blessing and liberation not a crime,
Helping unify sisters throughout history and time.
It's a garment of the believer from a faith sublime,
As evidently expressed in this short little rhyme.

Mother

Blessed am I to have the love of my mother,
Irreplaceable and unique is she like no other.
For me she went through the pain of birth,
She is ever precious to me within the earth.

My mother, she helped me to develop and grow,
She taught me wisdom and much I did not know.
My mother helped to make me the one I've become,
She gave me inner strength when I needed to overcome.

She taught me about Allah Most High above,
She helped me walk on the path of the faith I love.
Blessed by Allah - under her feet does lie paradise,
Her status is high in Islam – though not all realise.

My mother tried to make me smile when I was down,
She taught me appreciation and not to frown.
She taught me how to talk, laugh and walk on life's way,
She has been my supporting pillar each and every day.

Mothers are the pillar and cornerstone of the family,
Liberated by Islam, not enslaved but always free.
More precious then sparkling diamonds, rich rubies and gold,
Their love, strength and presence can't be sold.

Precious Mother

Dear Mother to me you gave birth,
God gifted in you precious life on earth.
You gave me all of your special time,
You even worshipped Allah The Sublime.

You fed me of your own blessed milk,
I pray for you heaven & wearing its silk.
In hunger you gave me my full feed,
You were there for whatever I did need.

Motherhood is a bestowed honour,
With all its blessings these ponder.
She is a companion, carer & friend,
Pray she sees me from birth till end.

To every child mum is beautiful,
Devoted to God & family is dutiful.
The Prophets had great mothers,
So did the best amongst the others.

Honoured for nine months with baby,
Adoption and fostering for others maybe.
Motherhood taught you to love,
Recognition of the All-Loving above.

They are heroines & they multi-task,
The pious do as Allah of them ask.
God gifted to her body do you emanate,
Show her respect and don't be ingrate.

A mother is the child's first teacher,
The one that teaches deen a preacher.
Heaven does lie beneath her feet,
She hears your little heartbeat.

It's inexpressible by words alone,
The love and values she has sewn.
To see you as you have now grown.
She loves you rightfully as her own.

Marriage, Love & Divorce

Marriage is considered an important Sunnah (practice of the Prophet). To the extent that he stated its fulfilment results in the completion of half of a believers faith and that in the other half they should fear their Lord. All of the Prophets married in their lifetime with the exception of Isa (pbuh) who will marry in his second coming. The marriage ideal is to be encompassed and premised on divine love that leads to humans humbling each other, showing love, care and affection. The Prophet never raised his hand to any of his wives; he helped in the house and treated them fairly. He taught that the one who marries more than one woman and fails to treat them equally will be raised with half their faculties paralysed. He taught:

'The most perfect believers are the best in conduct and the best of you are those who are best to their wives' (Ibn Hanbal).
'The most perfect believer in faith is the one whose character is finest and who is kindest to his wife.' (Tirmidhi and Nasa'i).

The Qur'an beautifully describes the protective bond between husband and wife as each have been made as a garment for each other. We know garments provide comfort, support, warmth and protection.

Marriage should not be forced or coerced in any shape or form since it removes the legitimacy of the marriage contract which is signed to bind husband and wife lawfully before God and the law.

Marriage is of huge importance as it fulfils half of one's faith. However there are clearly defined rules, principles, and conditions which need to be met to avoid unnecessary fallacies. The best example for us in this regard is Muhammad (p.b.u.h). He left his ummah with a wealth of information and dealt with the concerns of the ummah in this regard. It was central to the message of Muhammad (p.b.u.h) to liberate humans who were in bondage to ignorance and injustice.

Qadi Iyad in his Ash-Shifa states:

' 'A'isha, al-Hasan ibn 'Ali, Abu Sa'id al-Khudri and others described him. They said that he would work in the house with his family. He would delouse his clothes, mend his sandals, serve himself, sweep the house and hobble the camel. He would take the camels to graze and eat with the servants. He would knead bread with them and carry his own goods from the market.' (Kitab Ash-Shifa, Qadi 'Iyad Ibn Musa al-Yashubi, (Trans. Aisha Abdarrahman Bewley), 1999, p.68).

There are various types of love. God instils love and compassion into humans. Muslims believe Allah is Al-Wadud (All-Loving) and Ar-Rahman (The Compassionate). The greatest types of love a Muslim can have are Ishq Allah (love of God) and Ishq ay Rasul (Love of the Prophet). Frome these loves emanate the love of legitimacy, morality and they encompass your every doing. Divine love humbles and guides the believer aright.

Umm al Muminin Aisha (R.A) loved the Prophet (p.b.u.h) very much and would '…seek reassurances from him that he loved her. "How is your love for me?" she once asked. "Like the rope's knot," he replied, meaning that it was strong and secure. Many times after that she would ask, "How is the knot," and he would reply: " 'Ala halila"- "The same as ever!" ' (The wives of the Prophet Muhammad (s.a.w), Ahmad Thompson, p.79).

The Prophet (p.b.u.h) was a man of humility and treated his wives with respect and compassion. Umm al Mumineen (Mother of Believers) Aisha (R.A) recorded a sweet detail that indicated the Prophet's love: 'After I ate one part of the meat on a bone, I used to hand it down to the Prophet (SAW), who would bite the morsel from the place where I had bitten. Similarly, when I used to offer him something to drink after drinking a part, he would drink from the place I had put my lips.' (Muslim).

Divorce is most hated by Allah and rightfully so from all of the lawful things. As marriage is a sacred union where two people complete half of their faith. However, Allah out of His mercy circumstantially allowed divorce from either the husband or the wife. However, it is not a matter to be taken lightly and there are many rules and principles detailed in Islamic theology on this perennial issue. A man's pronouncement of divorce is called Talaq. A female's request for divorce is called Khula. In the timescale of the divorce is a waiting period for reconciliation and to see if there is a child born.

Islam doesn't cage marriage when oppression or injustice or infidelity takes place. However, marriage is preferred and love within that marriage should emanate from the greatest types of love Ishq Allah and Ishq ay Rasul.

Marriage - Zawj

United with affection, mercy, compassion & love,
A constant blessing for them both from high above.
Unity through marriage is beautifully celebrated,
Completion of half of faith means 2 are elevated.

With choice & agreement they're united by nikah,
A blessing of unity & emulation of the sunnah.
Strengthening righteousness & good in the Ummah.
As man & woman unite as decreed by Allah.

The nikah is conducted by both agreed with choice,
No coercion is permitted as both have a voice.
With 2 witnesses & an imam both sign the contract,
A document binding for a lifetimes full impact.

The Mahr, a gift is given from groom to the bride,
As in matrimony happily both man & woman are tied.
Thereafter the Walima a feast is given to the gathering,
To celebrate & share with others this unique blessing.

Both are made like a garment for one another,
United as one for security, warmth, protection & cover.
Mercy & love are instilled in hearts for tranquility,
Allah has endowed us all with having such an ability.

From all things lawful by Allah divorce is most hated,
As with marriage ½ deen is complete & Sunnah emulated.
Bound through Nikah husband & wife have a connection,
Unto one another like a garment of love & protection.

Now they are to live & traverse together on life's test,
Guided by the Qur'an & Sunnah the path that's best.
To overcome obstacles as sojourning on life's quest,
To live harmoniously with love of faith that's blessed.

Completing half of faith

There is someone, out there for whom in our inmost and hearts we all care,
Whatever they themselves feel, we know that Allah (SWT) is aware.
Love guided spiritually on the Prophetic path leads you to success,
This is a story about two who marry and love in this poem I express.

A young girl she was once and into a lady now she beautifully grew,
Her dream of marital completion and faith lived with words: 'I do'.
A young boy he was once and into a man now so handsome he grew,
His eyes sparkled with the hope of marriage to the one he but knew.

A man of a very high calibre and spiritual standing was he indeed,
A life of good faithfulness became his way and morals he did breed.
He was in past lost in ways so unworthy of his pathway that he changed,
Questions arose in his mind to purpose and hence his life was rearranged.

A woman who was quintessentially Islamic had she in time become,
A life so lowly she was not flamboyant and was only known to some.
In former times she was immature and childish in her worldly life,
Her company was of no help and would aid in causing others strife.

Both suffered the pangs of loneliness in a world that had become wrong,
But both doves would fly in each others wings in marriage not after long.
He proposed to her and went down upon his knees and wept in joy,
He told her that he was a rightful companion and not a little young boy.

A woman whose heart is not easily won she gave his words some thought.
She thought about her life and ways and what blessings he has brought.
She cried and said "Oh Allah, let not rivers of tears flow from such a heart,
Oh Allah fulfil me with the one from whom I won't ever in my life depart."

A man whose thoughts were no longer left in mind opened a new way,
His gratitude was to Allah and his future companion who'd light the day.
He cried and said "Oh Allah hear and answer this prayer and plea,
Of the hearts of those so strong and pure that wish to sail to their destiny."

Impatience was not the mind which prayed for countless days and nights,
But grace was ever deepening the dreams and senses of two shining lights.
He prayed "Oh Allah please may the day of joy and glory come to be,
Let my companion and I have a feeling and sight that we do not yet see".

The path that was deen al-Islam required this contract for its completion,
Any former ways and wrongs were apologised for and given a deletion.
In marriage both hearts had blossomed like a rose collecting rain drops,
they were completed with sincere affection imbued with faith that never stops.

To doubts were said "May Allah guide our wavering hearts to what is right,
Place us so firmly on the path so beautiful that's covered with spiritual light.
Let us be in a marriage of peace and bliss protected from any type of fight,
Give us in marriage the one whose compassion will protect each day and night."

My love, My Spouse

You are my star & my wings that take me high,
You are like my rainbow and bright lit blue sky.

You are my heart beat and you are my love,
A heavenly gift from the Ar-Rahman above.

You are my rose with a beautiful fragrance,
In faith we unite without any complacence.

You are unique with a powerful warm smile,
In marriage goodness truly is worthwhile.

You are the fulfilment in life to keep me well fed,
You are the star shining bright to guide me ahead.

My love & companion, strong together are we,
You are my lantern that rises above the sea.

A gentleman with mannerisms do you convey,
You turn the darkness in life into a new day.

Woman is the true compliment of every man,
A warm embracing love; to the suns heat my fan.

You are my flying carpet that roams the sky,
You are the wings of intimacy & love that we fly.

Radiant husband and dedicated companion of mine,
Your love draws me increasingly to the divine.

Serenity is the path we build upon and walk,
So humbled in awe and infatuated with your talk.

You are my night and shining armour, tough,
You protect me as I am in life your true love.

Together we surpass the love of Layla and Majnun,
United we are like the sky surrounding the moon.

Completion of Sunnah with you and half of my deen,
Our experiences are profound like a beautiful dream.

An Ode from a Queen to her King

What brings two much love & affection?
Marriage & faith a beautiful connection.

A Queen expressed this eloquently,
to her King as follows evidently.

As precious diamonds one can't forget,
Likewise the loving tale of this couplet.

"You're the one for me there is no question,
You're my completion and connection.

I am the candle and you are my flame,
Together bound by love we are the same.

You are the rose and I your petals bright,
You are the sunshine and I your beaming light.

The energy of love casts away any pain,
Showers us with happiness the lovers' rain.

Hands held the gaps in life we together fill,
Marriage so strong and firm, sunnah we fulfil.

Amazing grace of God pours over this place,
The place is the heart that none can erase.

My radiant King your presence encapsulates me,
Our bond traverses the oceans and sea.

Your smile is warm and your embrace serene,
You are the reality that I would only dream.

We were empty and now in marriage complete,
This love is eternal, non from the heart can delete.

Bound are we to the rules of love and legitimacy,
Not criminal in our encounters but in marital free.

Please keep for ever this love for life I've sent to you,
Our compassion is strong, warm in heart and but true.

We signed a contract and both became complete,
Now upon the throne you forever earn your seat.

I only asked once the chance of you and me,
You the one affirmed this love and mutuality."

Types of Ishq (Love)

Ishq (Love)

Love is a candle, love is a light,
It takes you onto a new height.
Love makes you humanly true,
It brings out the very best in you.
Love masters over values of hate,
It develops your spiritual state.
Love connects all and still unifies,
Love is God and the devil we despise.

Ishq Allah (Love of Allah)

Deeply imbued and immensely in love,
To God who is near and yet up above.
Blessings of which with I am smitten,
Spiritually Fulfilled thus been written.
Love encompassing all around you,
Compassionate Lord is evidently true.
His love is expressed in title Al-Wadud,
He loves those with his mention imbued.

Ishq ay Rasul (Love of the Prophets)

Love of the Prophets is ever great,
Teaching faith and ways to liberate.
An honouring of humanity's great men,
Love is their way, their writ & their pen.
Loving the exemplars leads you to God,
They are the upright guides & squad.
They are the greatest lovers in society,
Loving them and God leads you to piety.

Ishq dunya (Worldy love)

Hindered is the soul from its goal,
Faith & vicegerents was the role.
False love that often does misguide,
From God its love you can't hide.
You can love the good of this life,
Like your faith, fam, hubby or wife.
The dunya is a test extremely vast,
Yearn for the akhira like those of past.

Divorce most hated

God loves marriage sweet of a Sunnah complete,
Half of deen accomplished after the marital seat.
To remain steadfast & happy together as decided,
Use your inner strength & ensure you're never divided.

From all lawful things divorce is the most hated,
Since in marriage is a unity for two souls liberated.
Through marriage with ½ of faith already done,
The rest with Taqwa & compassion will be won.

This life is a trial so you're all bound to be tested,
The best had many & worked arduously – rarely rested.
Striving through trials & tribulations ensures success,
On Yawm ul Qiyamah your account will be addressed.

There are doubts that at times say divorce times 3,
That naseeha may be misguided imprisonment not free.
So remain together & counsel it through & through,
Since with the Sunnah be kind - goodness will imbue.

When a document was signed signatures were two,
Of the blessings of Allah for bride, groom tis true.
Guests overjoyed with feasts & what was given,
Don't let marriage break – let situations be forgiven.

Since a situation may appear but not as shown,
To the Creator the framing & gaming is known.
Doubts may be untruths that the honest know,
The crooks against marriage break the flow.

Marriages can be strong if to truth they're bound,
Choices should be made on character if clearly sound.
But not on rumours & division of opportunities arisen,
But what is destiny using logic, through and reason.

Divorce is most hated but allowed as a final resort,
In situations like violence when both have fought.
Also if it was not out of their choice but forced,
Since my Lord loves mercy and not the coerced.

When something's made it's destined to be together,
Liked when united through seasons & every weather.
Divorce hated for the break & difficulty it brings,
Despite the effort of planning marriage & all things.

Loving the one destined to you will make it strong,
To ensure there is right, justice then doing wrong.
Remember Allah is watching all you say and do,
The decipherer of what is a test of false and true.

Along the journey of life and death

Muslims believe that this life is a test. They believe that life is created by Allah with the key purpose of His Worship. Life is considered a sacred gift from Allah and should be protected and treated well as it is an amanah (trust). Muslims believe that children are a blessing and are little miracles that emerge from the womb of a mother.

Muslims believe that the one guarantee you have at the inception of your life due to your finite nature is that you will die and cease to exist. They believe that the angel Azrail will take your soul at the time of death. This will be either gently for the good doers or harshly for the wrongdoers. They believe in a life after death that includes the questioning of the grave, resurrection, Judgement Day and the entry into either the abode of hell or heaven.

Loving Child – Praises from mothers

As I saw you come and enter my world,
The adhan were the words you first heard.
Your little soft hands and eyes so bright,
In my life you brought me immense light.

Overjoyed your father and I have become,
Fortunate to conceive as its gift comes only to some.
You grappled my hand and never did leave,
You were the perfect gift from Allah I've received.

It was difficult for me to give you birth on that day,
But the joys you bring were worth it in every way.
My child I love you for being the one, who is nice,
You followed Allah's path and never did any vice.

When you came into this world you were so small,
I watched you in your crib and soon you did but crawl.
Sometimes you would walk, run and often fall.
But you grew up and responded to Allah's call.

How proud can a mother be with such respect?
It baffles me how any life one can ever reject?
I reminisce when you would often give up and cry,
But my loving child you succeeded each time you'd try.

Your precious nature I was entrusted with here,
Even if you move away, in my heart you'll always be near.
If I were ever to lose you how empty my life would be,
I'm so proud of you to be an extraordinary part of me.

Little miracles - Blessings in disguise

Precious little babies enter the fold of iman,
Upon hearing the blessed call of the adhan.
Blessed with this miraculous special gift,
Many feel overwhelmed and happily uplift.

Overjoyed are we as the aqiqah is celebrated,
Another wonderful sunnah is thus emulated.
The baby is given Tahneek something sweet,
For this blessing to be good that we all greet.

From non-existence these little hearts beating,
With life and a future of a mumin believing.
It's presence ineffable for joy we're receiving.
A light of goodness on us that's now beaming.

The baby cries for hunger a mother understands,
Giving it comfort & grappling its gentle hands.
It's amazing growth in time one comprehends,
As with a newly addition the ummah expands.

The babies open their eyes to a world never seen,
Seeing a giggle & happy countenance many dream,
Husband & wife with this new addition to the team,
With this small miraculous blessing from Al-Haleem.

It's formation attests to Allah's magnificence,
Conferred with a name of spiritual significance.
Created with complex mechanisms & benevolence,
It's care, upbringing and teaching is of relevance.

An ode to Tahir

Tahir a sweet loving and gifted friend,
a blessing in disguise, he was a God send.

He was always loving, considerate and kind,
a humble one who always had others on his mind.

In Bradford he was a radiant beaming light,
he always strived and held to what is right.

He memorised the Qur'an off by heart,
He was blind but this was his spirits art.

He was an exemplar, who still had studied,
To help others in need he always had hurried.

He always passed with kind words and a smile,
any encounter in his presence was worthwhile.

Unlike many others his persona was unique,
amazing and gifted with how he would speak.

All those he encountered he would greet,
made the most out of life with every heartbeat.

A bro who was simple and filled with humility,
he led a life filling others with a deep serenity.

His dedication shone as he was always motivated,
now gone to Allah in peace, finally liberated.

May he always rest in peace.

Little innocent child

An amazing child that I knew was ever so sweet,
Allah had taken her soul upon that final heartbeat.
I hoped that once again inshallah we could meet.

We wished we were all there right by her side.
An innocent child with a beautiful smile wide,
She had so much hope and always had tried,

Heart breaking was the news to the end of her life,
Little did many know of her struggle and strife,
Her pain made life quite difficult and rife.

She was a small child that became terminally ill,
Who nevertheless remained determined still.
Yet we know the time of death is at Allah's will.

She was suffering in pain from a form of cancer,
At the time chemotherapy was the best answer.
But hopefully in Jannah was a place made for her.

In School she was a small radiant beaming light,
A child who strived and tried to do what's right.
Until the end with hope & courage she did fight.

To her friends she was a loving and gifted friend,
A blessing in disguise, she was a little God send.
Her death for many was a reason for them to mend.

When we lost her our hearts entrenched with sorrow,
Thinking she would still be back with us tomorrow,
Lessons from her hope we could all humbly borrow.

We wish her so much happiness & hereafter of bliss,
Knowing her families prayers and loss with a final kiss,
Her presence in our hearts is ever so sorely missed.

How hard it was for her mother to gently let her go,
Often the sorrows and pain can still be long and slow,
But back to Allah are we all really destined we know.

A little girl who was simple and filled with humility,
She had led a life filling many with much serenity,
Her being continually missed is really for us a surety.

Little child innocent - Allah took away your pain,
May Allah shower you with blessings that remain,
I pray may we all meet in heaven inshallah again.

May your memory remind us that life is but a test,
Wishing for you in barzakh and the hereafter the best,
May you in serenity and God's grace peacefully rest.

By your side my friend

Right from the beginning to the end,
A gift of prayer and peace I send.
Always right by your side my friend,
There's still time for us to help & mend.

Don't give up or live in life with fear,
God counts your every word and tear.
Always ever close and ever so near,
Your smile hides the pain you inhere.

I know deep down your in much pain,
Cruelly suffering over & over again,
Yet patiently little do you complain,
Even though life's no longer the same.

But I know your wounds will heal,
Your faith in this test remains real.
As to Allah you pray to & kneel,
Sending salam on Prophethood's seal.

The testing trials have been very long,
But my friend for you I keep strong.
No matter how much we know it's wrong,
It is to Allah we all return and belong.

So many memories I do reminisce,
Our great times friend I deeply miss.
I pray for your life and after with bliss,
Sealed with duas to you I dedicate this.

Death

Creeping slowly and covering me completely like a tidal wave is death's call.
No escape from it do we all have from metal barriers or even a barricaded wall.
Resonating is its sound and its movement like a shadow behind my very life,
The one who is good will feel gentleness & those who did wrong will feel strife.

Yet death is something that can also be so peaceful like a feather floating in the air,
Taken so gently from the arms of my bed in my sleep, to the angel of death there.
No excuse can I give and no time can I expect to amend my ways and use of time.
When the call comes – there is no way out as we go back to the call of the divine.

Death, how cruel it seems to hear death from bombs and blood to wailing screams,
But how cruel it is, we waste this opportunity to fulfil material goals and dreams.
How many people have gone before us who thought this world would be forever,
But this is not something you or I can escape with any type of human endeavour.

Death is part of a journey that spans from the very moment lives are conceived,
It is the news given at birth that is essential to our purpose and must be received.
Death is like the mortal enemy of those who haven't taken heed in this life now,
But death is like the friend of the righteous who submitted to Allah and did bow.

Death is ever so real but often so blind to our sight with which we see the world,
Death is like a sound whose very presence causes the body to shiver by its word.
It reminds you of the dark gallows and dungeons – the loneliness it brings to you.
It reminds you of the emptiness of the bodies filled with former life with no clue.

Is it not the case that we often only reflect about our mistakes only in hindsight?
With great certainty then I must part from the worldly love diminishing the light.
In our worldly aspirations we become filled with desires and forget our purpose.
But death cries faith and simplicity as the pathways for any type of recompense.

Who is the friend of death – is it those sunken in the depths of pain and despair?
Who is the very enemy of death – the righteous ones immersed in Zikr and care?
But the loud thunderbolt of death with its light surpassing is indiscriminate on all.
Death does not come only to sick, old, terminally ill but spans from old to small.

Who will vindicate the life of the one that slowly passes by each minute and day?
Who will heed the silent cry of the one who prostrates for forgiveness each day?
It is but now that the search begins for seeking the truth in life my dearest friend.
Heed the message that birth gave to you – with life comes one guarantee, an end.

So as we reflect on passages of death we near our reflections and simple conclusion,
Just as life is real and temporal then belief in death is its corollary not some illusion.
Lives are like droplets of water in a great ocean that submerge and easily disappear.
So be prepared my friend as no moment is for fanciful waste as death is ever near.

Muslim Eschatology – signs before Qiyamah

Of the future warning the Prophet did prophesize,
He warned of what would in the future arise.
The exact time of the final hour is known to God,
The signs would probably have sounded odd.
Since they were events yet to have taken place,
Finding them through time hasn't been a chase.

Amongst the signs are some that are major,
Preceding them are signs that are minor.

Minor – women and men will dress equal,
Homosexuality will spread to this a sequel.
Fornication, killing, hypocrisy all widespread,
Zina a sin if married or not even yet wed.
Many leaders but few that will be honest as,
Countries respected of their brutality has.
30 false Prophets will come and appear,
Forging their own paths for people to adhere.
An increase in alcohol & drug addiction,
New diseases & sudden deaths arisen.
Faith will be sold cheaply for a small price,
People will be ignorant of Allah not wise.
Bedouins will compete in making buildings tall,
The signs show humans descent & from haqq fall.

Major – eclipses major there will be three,
Sun rising from the west you will see.
A huge smoke will arise in the sky,
A beast will come and speak to people aye.
Gog and Magog will wreak havoc much,
Mahdi will come and guide - a positive touch.
The anti-Christ Dajjal will come and appear,
Isa (Jesus) pbuh will fight him on earth here.
Dajjal will have an army of 70,000 Jews,
Kafir is written between his eyes – his bad news.
He will start conquering the world except two,
Madina and Makkah he can't enter - true.
Isa will kill Dajjal the false one eyed liar.
Judgement will come - heaven and the hell fire.

Signs were given a warning of the end of time,
Of what was to proceed as expressed in my rhyme.
Many minor signs have already come into fruition,
The Prophet had foresight, miracles and vision.

Eschatology

Call it fact or fiction psychology,
Truth is the unfolding eschatology.
So many symptoms & evident signs,
Wake up peeps were living in the times.
Global warming & many natural disasters,
Tsunamis, earthquakes yet ego masters.
Everything happening before our eyes,
Manifest reality you need to realise.
Eloquently reminded by the wise,
Not to be fooled by the Dajjal's lies.
A global awakening is much needed,
Lest death fall upon us whilst unheeded.
Warned by the Prophets of the end of time,
Not pondering & acting on it may be the crime.

Akhira

Muslims believe this life to be upon them a test,
Each will be judged on their wrong and their best.
To mislead them is the enemy of God – the devil,
He teaches disobedience and from faith to rebel.

Angel Azrail will at time of death take the soul,
You had the chance before this in life to extol.
Succeeding and reaching Allah was the end goal,
You had the Qur'an to guide & the Prophet's role.

The good their souls he'll remove very gentle,
The bad he will remove very hard detrimental.
The dead will see others weep at their casket,
The promised death came from birth at the basket.

Angels Munkar and Nakir will ask 3 questions,
In the grave none will give any suggestions.
They ask What is your religion? & Who is your Lord?
Who is your Prophet? Answer to this accord.

Those good who answer correctly will be at peace,
Those bad who didn't will suffer without any ease.
Except the children and those who are shuhadah,
Because they were innocent or said the Shahadah.

Until Judgement day they remain within this fate,
Then they will be resurrected in their original state.
For this Angel Israfil will blow his horn three times,
It's already mentioned in other types of rhymes.

It is a belief & guarantee that the world ceases,
Since My Lord is the decider & does as He pleases.
The signs before the day are on the increases,
The time for each person day by day decreases.

All will be judged upon their life and deeds,
Allah gave us Qur'an and Sunnah to fulfil our needs.
The righteous are the inheritors of a place illiyin,
The wrongdoers are the inheritors a place sijjin.

Azrail – Takes the soul at death
Barzakh – State of waiting & questioning in grave
Israfil – Will sound horn three times
Book of Deeds – Book of all your deeds written by angels on shoulders
Mizan – Deeds will be weighed on a balance
Sirat – A bridge will be crossed to go heaven or fall into hell
Jannah – The abode of the righteous and the rewarded
Jahannam – The abode of the wrongdoers who'll be punished

Jannah (Heaven)

Heaven is an abode of wonders and delights,
For those who reached the highest heights.
In it there will be no death or ceasing of life,
It will be free of pain, anguish and strife.

The righteous are inheritors of heaven,
Of which there are layers in total of seven.
Above the seventh heaven is Allah,
Met by Muhammad (pbuh) given salah.

Seven levels are Firdaws, Dar-us Salam
Jannat al- Adn, mentioned in hadith Kalam,
There is also Jannat-an Naim, Dar-ul Khlud,
Jannat-ul Mawa, and Illiyyun for the good.

Angels will present you with a mansion,
Your rewards will increase in expansion.
It will have rivers, gardens and light,
It will be a place of happiness not fright.

Sweeter than honey and whiter than milk,
Kauthar and the wearing of the luxury silk.
You'll be reunited with your lost deceased,
Only if they attained heaven as He pleased.

Palaces with rivers flowing beneath,
Protection from Hell and its heavy heat.
There will be Silver and crystal dishes,
Rewards manifold as Allah upon you wishes.

It is a place of purity, peace and contentment,
Beauty, happiness and many more element.
The Prophets are in Firdaus the highest in paradise,
They were God fearing, spiritual and really wise.

There are eight gates of Jannah to be won,
Baabus Salah is for those that their prayer done.
Baabal Jihad for those who in God's way fought,
Baabus Sadaqah for the charitable who God sought.
Baabul Rayyan for those who observed the fast,
Baabul Hajj for those who go on pilgrimage as asked.
Baabul Kaazimeenal Ghaiz Wal Aafina Anin Nas,
For those that pardon others and suppress anger as.
Baabul Aiman is for those saved from chastisement,
Baabuz Zikr for those that remember Allah as meant.

To enter these gates you must excel in each,
Follow and emulate what the Prophet did teach.
You will then be saved and have a high reach,
The reward is individual to all persons each.

To Allah one should pray and implore,
If it is a heavenly abode they yearn for.
Seek forgiveness and piety to gain more,
Be subordinate to God and in His awe.

Jahannam (Hell)

Hell is an abode given to humans as a punishment,
Those who disobeyed Allah receive this detriment.
The fire of hell is hotter than human known heat,
It is the abode of rejection where pain you meet.

Those who fought against Allah will this receive,
As will those who committed sin & did not believe.
The punishments bring much fear and nightmares,
Its magnitude and its various elements scares.

In hell you receive shoes with hot boiling water,
Unlike Heaven and the sweet and white Kauthar.
It is a place of no escape but heavy torment,
It is a place unbelievers will be punished & sent.

The most wretched will be sent in this abode,
The Heavy rocks on the heads will implode.
In the heat skin will be re-given & skin will burn
It will be a place not even the worst will yearn.

There are snakes and scorpions that will sting,
Nothing other than your deeds will you bring.
Boiling liquid will be drink & poured on you,
Clothes will be made of burning sulphur tis true.

Those who fell of (sirat) the bridge will enter,
They will receive punishment from a tormentor.
After a long time the Angels will let some free,
Those who have some faith & goodness we see.

The decision from Barzakh till Qiyamah is ongoing.
For those who were wicked, evil and wrongdoing
Those who attested Shahadah will eventually leave,
For the others their rejection is reason to grieve.

There are many sins coated sweet that Satan lures,
He removes the protection and your future cures.
He wrongs & misleads as do his helpers -humankind,
In listening to him eventual abyss and hell we find.

Those who commit suicide their death will repeat,
Since life belongs to Allah and non can compete.
Hell has a tree called Zaqqum which will be food,
A taste of pain for those whose sins had accrued.

Hell has seven gates for differing situations,
Prophets warned of its abode to all their nations.
The first gate is Jahannam whose fire will scorch,
Heavy punishment and pain as it will torch.
The 2nd gate is Ladha – fire will eat body parts,
Diminishing kidneys, stomachs and hearts.
The 3rd is Saqar where fire will eat only their flesh,
The punishments are continued starting afresh.
The 4th gate is Al-Hutamah it will shatter the bones,
None will intervene no matter how much one moans.
The 5th gate is Jaheem which is one big coal,
A place of heat for the one who wronged the soul.
The 6th gate is Sa'eer as it is constantly kindling,
Filled with snakes, scorpions, ropes etc not ending.
The 7th is Al-Hawiyah – he who enters never leaves,
A warning and punishment the sinner grieves.

Zabaniyah are the angels that will punish with Malik,
For those forgot to submit to Allah who is Al-Khaliq.
To avoid this abode one must follow the guide,
Choices are given as we have free-will to decide.

Peace, Justice & Conflict

Islam is a religion that is rooted in the term peace. One of the divine names of Allah is As-Salam (The All Peace). Allah likes peace and peacemakers and hates the starters of war. Nevertheless, Allah states in the Qur'an "Fight in the cause of Allah those who fight you, but do not transgress limits; for Allah loves not transgressors." (Qur'an: 2:190). The Prophet was a peaceful man but in the face of brutes and war mongers he fought to defend himself and others. However, he made a constitution, treaties and pacts and preferred peace and harmony over war.

Muslims have clearly defined rules for defence which include not harming the innocent, not destroying earth, and much more. The Qur'an enjoins peace-making *"And if they incline towards peace, incline thou also towards it, and put thy trust in Allah. Surely it is He Who is All-Hearing All-Knowing."* (Qur'an: 8:62). However, the greatest struggle for a believer is to fight their own ego and strive in the way of Allah. This is called Jihad al-Akbar whereby Muslims struggle everyday of their life to be better people.

Muslims believe that Allah is Al-Adl (The Just) and that His laws are just. Muslims believe divine justice supersedes all types of justice. Since He is Al-Aleem (All-Knowing) everything is within his knowledge and therefore Muslims believe we should have tawakkul (trust) in Allah.

Across the world humans suffer injustice at the hands of tyrannies. Muslims suffer injustice and oppression across the world, whether it is from their own governance or from wars and occupations from colonisers and more powerful nations. Some of these countries include Burma, Palestine, Syria, Iraq, Afghanistan etc. To this injustice is the need for a peaceful uprising with the help and support of people across the world so that they no longer wail and mourn the death of their people and nations, but sing peace at the revitalisation of their people and nations.

The occupiers
Horrendous is the screaming and the wailing of death and destruction,
As superpowers exploit in the name of freedom and globalisation.
Wars are created, but I will certainly not allow them in my name,
Strategic interests, money and power hunger are their only game.

But they can't expect people to silently accept exploitation's flame,
Conflicts are double sides or more because injustice is to blame.
Modern Pharaoh's of the world, they worship their wealth and fortune,
But Allah has warned them as Allah diminishes the unjust very soon.

The sanctity of life so innocent for which they don't care or preserve,
But Allah compensates those lives in heaven the innocent's reserve.
Mother's raped and dishonoured lose their children, and wives their men,
Yet people recall with the holocaust an empty cry 'never again'.

Bosnia, the scars and bereavement we will never from our memories forget,
Stand up for justice and for the love of God we'll make no regret.
The silence of Europe and many other powers was truly shocking,
But for no Muslim on earth are these events for the blocking.

Kashmir, we hear your screams from the occupation of India,
All the crimes are covered up by the silent propaganda and media.
But Azad you shall be with strength, everlasting faith and belief,
It is Allah and those who surrender to His will that will give relief.

Palestine, Israel can no longer continue to commit its crimes silently,
Have the descendants of the holocaust forgotten their deaths by Hitler violently?
Al Quds will not be destroyed by their wealth, prestige and power,
Remember what is taking place is a clear portent of the last hour.

Chechnya, your freedom you fight from Russia's aggression,
But don't let their tactics become like Beslan a horrible obsession.
Keep strong brothers and sisters in times so rough with tribulation,
Who do they have? When we have the Prophet as our guide, the best of all creation.

Afghanistan remember you were once financed to fight the Soviet threat,
Now the CIA has put that in the past and plunders you – we won't forget.
In the name of the war on terror they sent many to Guantanomo,
This is their free world – that's where they wouldn't themselves go.

Iraq, you were plundered not for freedom from Saddam, but your oil,
Illegally on lies were you occupied and Abu Ghraib was on your soil.
Pained by sanctions your basic necessities are no longer replete,
But from history this illegal aggression with dodgy dossiers, they can't delete.

Muslim Ummah wake up and heed those things that are wrong,
Don't be deluded in the Dajjalic system filled with so much wrong.
Faith will certainly serve so hard as a testing trial,
As freedoms are stolen and Orwellian times are fulfilled with denial.

"The Muslim Ummah is one body, where one part feels the pain so does the rest." (Hadith)

Palestine
A beautiful blessed place is Palestine
A land of Prophets from the divine.
Abraham's (a.s) descendants see crime,
Perpetrated by Israel time after time.

A land important for all of the Ummah,
Filled for every prayer & Jummah.
In Al-Aqsa the Prophet led all the ambiya,
Sent through the heavens on Buraq to Allah.

Occupied are people in their own land,
As the walls of this apartheid expand.
Asking for Peace & security a demand.
Yet their rights violated and slammed

Herzl said the land was empty then,
I ask his followers as of this when?
Forgetting your lives & existence again.
Like second class citizens it's insane.

Genocide lessons must be for all time.
The Nazis committed a heinous crime,
You shouldn't suffer this same fate,
Filled with injustice and the same hate.

The truth the Israelis try to deny,
Blaming you for this crime is a lie.
Wiped from the globe as you die,
I hear your pain & increasing cry.

As each argues they are more logical.
This is more than just psychological.
Dimensions are religious as well as political.
As it relays much of the eschatological,

The two state solution seem to be blank,
Only the Gaza strip and the West Bank,
If not already bulldozed by another tank.
Already bombarded the plan has sank.

Sanctions are already taking their toll,
Stopped & harassed your lives are stole.
Asking is your annihilation their goal,
When you equally all have in you a soul.

All the tears and anguish in your eyes,
Asking why no-one hears your daily cries.
Yet so many of you care on both sides,
Hating this bloodshed and these tides.

Progeny of Prophets please live in peace,
Lift these burdens and give all the ease.
The ego betrays so to it don't appease,
As many die praying upon their knees.

When children are bombed when they play,
Shelters are ruined with nowhere to stay.
To be compensated on Judgement day.
Victory for those walking on Allah's way.

Palestine – I hear your cry!

The land was blessed with the Prophetic Temple,
As Solomon (a.s) & David (a.s) led by example.
A land that was never empty but always ample.
With miracles of which Al-Aqsa is a living example.

Since 2000 al-Quds we've seen the second Intifada,
Children defending with stones West Bank & Gaza.
Murdered are memories as living gets much harder.
As this human tragedy develops into a big disaster.

Many are marked with shrapnel wounds and scars,
They keep strong in this nightmare like little stars.
Not surprisingly they are psychologically affected,
As they relive these dark nightmares daily enacted.

We can't forget Ariel Sharon the butcher of Beirut,
Plundered Sabra & Shatila innocents they did shoot.
Olive trees uprooted and destroyed are their fruit,
As the Palestinians see their lives and land uproot.

They're impeded by the apartheid wall and barricades,
Israel's wish from the map of earth Palestine fades.
In a land that was a refuge for the Pharaoh's slaves,
Sadly are increasing many innocent people's graves.

Deprived by economic embargos and sanctions,
In a land with warring and dividing of factions.
Israel is very aware of their deliberate actions,
Not surprising are the protests & many reactions.

Daily harassment and identity checks on the roads,
Having to sadly subordinate to the occupiers codes.
Is it not wrong to kill and maim the innocent souls?
By sharing and caring you can fill the gaps and holes.

Based on this greed and injustice to cause attrition,
We saw many unholy alliances in a built up coalition.
From their own land they're given a notice of eviction,
As 'The Goyim' bashing and killing became addiction.

We've seen Camp David, Oslo & other agreements,
Never fulfilled when there's so many impediments.
As every day another sorrow it's people laments,
We need change not simple rhetorical sentiments.

The holy land should not have to be desecrated,
For the righteous and faithful will all be elevated.
A dream for peace and freedom is long awaited.
I pray for the day when they will all be liberated,

Syria & Burma

They ask what is all this hype and hysteria?
We all lament it's a war in the land of Syria.
Oh beautiful blessed land of the Shaam,
How could you have come to much harm?

The land that Isa (a.s) will emerge from,
Has been riddled with injustice and scum.
A land that produced a vault of scholars,
Fought for the greed of wealth & dollars.

Many nations involved in bombardment,
Forgotten not to kill in the commandment.
Cities turned into rubble, dust and ash,
Brigands in high places thinking of cash.

Burma how could the nightmare unfold,
Surely Buddhists adhere to peace told.
How could so many civilians now arise?
Is it their faith or culture you despise?

Many have been sent to Bangladesh,
Like Jahiliyah thoughts are still fresh.
Lies and rumours sparked a conflict,
Every Muslim passed as a convict.

The Rohingya have become displaced,
At the hands of the Burmese disgraced.
Ethnic cleansing we've heard it before,
It needs to end Nil is its clear score.

How much more in this world is there turmoil?
Wars from superpowers for greed & oil.
Plots from fools they try to unfoil,
Both are unjust it makes my blood boil.

How many refugee camps in the world?
How from riches has poverty unfurled?
Innocence weeps, wails and seizes,
My Lord wants justice do as He pleases.

War Child

A stranger and lonely mother do I feel in this darkened world,
Present I am, but the pain & anguish within me lives & goes unheard.
Relentless humans cause my river of tears to submerge into an ocean.
Lost is humanity in its wrong materialistic and selfish devotion.

My innocent child you killed and took away from me,
To wars with bombs & soldiers that brought pain and misery.
My child I bore, took care of & was blessed within my womb,
Now scattered into pieces brought alone together in a tomb.

Oh murderer how can your greed occupy your heart so much,
You took away innocence and justice with one deadly touch.
Who called you to come and destroy my beautiful world?
Lies and rumours that were misguided – that's all you heard!

I am a human, a mother with love lost, in despair, left in need,
But I have the deep hope my child is happy as a shaheed.
My joy, my happiness you turned so easily into death the enemy's pride,
Behind these cold layers of falsehood they cannot always hide.

How long can you say that the world will be resolved in killing?
The ingredients of peace, equality & justice are better fulfilling.
With the uncertainties of war toppled with lies there is no winning,
You've got to free all of humanity from such shackles of sinning.

Each day a new wound seems to open within me inside,
The animosity is completely wrong – where can I hide?
Why with your treachery are games played on my mind?
The answer is look at history – it's the same I will find.

Mercy will rain on innocence and heal its every wound and scratch,
Oh unjust oppressor, murderer of my child you will be given your match.
Injustice – your time will always diminish & certainly end,
Remember the day of reckoning and the angel of death Allah will send.

My child I hope one day we will be together again,
Soothed from the wounds with endless tears and ongoing pain.
I hope we will all stand shoulder to shoulder in time,
An example to humanity of compassion of a value sublime.

Poverty

The world you once loved is lost before your eyes,
Immersed in your emotions from situations you despise.
Stolen is your happiness by a life of devastation,
Slavery has shackled your freedom and liberation.

The dreams you longed for are challenged by war,
Your avenues of happiness are curtailed seem no more.
Tears fall down your innocent little face,
Your loved ones before your eyes are now erased.

Your shelter ruined by another natural disaster,
Your freedom's stolen by politicians that master.
Emotions take over as you're filled with despair,
The world sleeps silently to the devil's snare.

Globalisation the vision once given as an opportunity,
Yet used by unjust oppressors with impunity.
Encroached are your rights to bare necessities,
Stolen are your belongings and loved amenities.

Poverty it wails with the sighs of deep pain,
It is the sacrifice of humanity to no gain.
LEDC's are crippled by exorbitant rates of interest,
Decisions are made with no consideration of the rest.

Poverty requires elimination from our world,
With the collective goodwill of action and word.
Soothe the wounds, devastation, tears and pain,
Let dreams of happiness and peace live again.

We know

We know the injustices of the times,
So with our voices upbeat lyrics and rhymes,
We make melodies exposing the crimes.

Our innocent peeps suffering the wars,
When in sickness they are dying for cures.
When Pharaoh's be breaking the doors.

It's getting harder but we keep going,
We got to keep the justice flowing.
We know the discontent they be sowing.

We don't need power & prestige for show,
When we aim high to Allah and not low.
You know brethren the path does flow.

We seeing the hate and the pains,
The mouth silenced & heart that complains,
For victory & mercy & its rains.

We seeing da mind games and magic,
We know this travesty is truly tragic,
Don't get induced coz it's like static.

Families and friends being divided,
Breaking the trusts once confided.
To this we know we can't be sided.

Tears rolling down and turning into blood,
The rivers and oceans turning into mud,
You are seeing a division from a former bud.

But we got to keep the light shining,
To the truth we all need to be signing,
Keep the hope when they rather we be whining.

Victory to the brothers and sisters,
The faith of the new peaceful resistance,
Of great times in history reminiscence.

Peace

(Chorus)
I sing the song of peace; I sing the song of peace.
My love and compassion is finally released.
I am freed from the shackles of persecution and pain,
I forgive you and leave on you no blame.

As children dance and smile once again they feel their freedom,
They reign in new opportunities in their chainless kingdom.
Their thirst is quenched and their hunger for freedom is filled,
Their broken hearts are fixed and their dreams finally fulfilled.

How beautiful is the sight of peace with the colours it brings.
Its joys are so much so – that they are filled with blessings.
Finally I can enjoy the noise not of bombs but of happiness,
I can rejoice to my Merciful Lord for this eventual bliss.

(Chorus)

Joyful joy and sugared thoughts so sweet reside deep within me,
I finally can dance to the tune of peace encompassing me.
There's so much grace I feel from my God above,
My answered prayers responded with compassion and love.

The scenery of rubble seems so beautiful free from war,
Each survivor I see increases my happiness more,
Free from shackles of impoverishment I'm filled with joy,
As smiles extend from man, woman, girl and every boy.

(Chorus)

The mothers who formerly wailed sing with their children peace,
From former times of hardship – they now feel inside the ease.
Families are united with no walls now dividing them apart,
Rekindled are they and strengthened deep in their heart.

Light fills the world once again with peace so serene and sweet,
When common human values are humbled – unity we do meet.
All happiness encompasses those darker times of anguish and pain,
As our hearts smile and feel the echoing of the peace again.

(Chorus)

Peace, so delightful, nice, ecstatic and all things good,
Finally humanity has come together as one neighbourhood.
Shared values and love are recipes of success,
The virtues that come in response are the best.

Forgiveness

Forgiveness is the requisite towards healing deep wounds and pain inside,
Iman gives tranquillity and nourishes your spirit with peace of mind.

Forgiveness Is the liberation from the pangs of wrong subdued in guilt,
It is the bricks of remorse and sincere amending of a new life to be built.

No human life can ever traverse on life's way without mercy and love,
Allah is the only infinite merciful forgiver who rains blessings from above.

Often in our short life so many wrongs we do commit and just despair,
But when in depths of hardship remember with Dhikr is true care.

No tear goes unnoticed by Allah who transcends and is Al-Aleem,
He blessed us with solutions from the exemplary way of the al-Amin.

Imperfection is our human nature so our mistakes will be a test and trial,
So have complete tawakkul in Allah and feel content and in hope just smile.

Holding grudges and closing the gate of forgiveness is common to us all,
But why be so unjust when in life we often succeed and so often also fall?

So I seek forgiveness for my worldly ways so easily led astray, please,
It's an open door to opportunity's closed door of relentlessness without peace.

So my Rabb forgive me as to you I prostrate and weep to on my knees, Release me from injustice, stagnation and subjection to much greater ease.

The vision

The greatest vision on earth was the vision that God had for humanity. This vision was transmitted by the angel Jibrail to the Prophets. The Prophets in turn were inspired by God and were visionaries for their nations. Muhammad (pbuh) was a visionary sent to all of humanity – his vision extended beyond his community. When in Medina he set up a constitution, laid the rules and boundaries for his community to thrive and survive. He gave the great Khutbah tul Hajja his final sermon and in that he articulated key points mentioned elsewhere in the book.

A child's cream is a visionary poem on the expectations of society and the ideals the child wishes to see. The poems on education are to inspire learners, educators and society in regards to education.

A child's dream

How often I would dream about
residing in a world filled with peace,
A world sewn ever so tight from
fragmentation and any form of unease.
A perfect world concocted in my little
mind like a seed that soon grows,
This seed develops into the branches
of perfection where order flows.

Reminiscing of the life I was once
born into of pampering and affection,
But now I ask such a painful question
why with growth is their rejection.
My eyes have now grown to see a
world with such immense magnitude.
Yet despite all I have I often fall
to the fallacy of human ingratitude.

My dream is not a dream of words
so blindly thought and fantasised,
Its rational reflection and heartfelt
mercy and faithful love realised.
I am not the child locked in the past, who
sees a world that does not exist,
I am the child of the future who
holds to justice and to wrong resist.

I have a vision not just kept in eyes but
extending to the plane of humanity,
That we are one people and must unite
to enhance our lives – that's reality!
Come embrace me and my words and
share my dream and make it true,
What is of benefit and envisioned is
not solely for me but also for you.

Great thinkers and people of thought
began with a dream like me the child,
Often laughed and ridiculed for speaking
nonsense but it's we that smiled.
Please hear my call and preserve this
world and regain its great beauty,
What we can all do is work collectively
and then fulfil our individual duty.

My dream is not a dream of thought
but feelings within my heart so deep,
So join with me on this treasure hunt
for peace in reality not in your sleep.
Tears, laughter, smiles, frowns and
many faces I have made as expression,
I have a vision for our progress and
change preserved from any regression.

My dream is one where humanity unite
to sing a song of God's praise,
A world where we spiritually join hands
together and for the good liaise.
My dream is the vision that brings
light to the darkness of our life,
It is the power of love covered with
self-sacrifice free of any strife.

Dreams may seem to begin in minds
and may be lost in thoughts within,
But this is the incentive to create the
steps of success in reality and win.
I am not the dreamer of the past then
whose life is marred from reality,
What I love so much is unity, justice,
truth and the sound of people free.

Visions emerge from little people so
insignificant in the eyes of others,
But strength develops like the formation
of cells to humans from mothers.
My dream is then not one of a former past,
but the voice for a future good,
I will aid its realisation from my heart to
flourish in any way that I could.

So have divine love my friend and dream
with me a vision so beautifully great,
Don't worry about delivery because we're
not restricted by any particular date.
My vision is a vision of love not consumed
in the fire of relentlessness and hate,
Join with me all dreamers and thinkers as
time is of the essence and we can't wait.

Let's dream together, live together and embrace the love and preservation of peace.

Education

In Hunger and need for liberation,
Quench this thirst with education.
Taking you to a much loftier station.
Giving with it the mind emancipation.

In a world filled with wars & guns blazing,
Phones, ipods & internet you're all crazing.
Wanting to be with the rest of the hood,
Forsaking knowledge & all that is good.

Why waste time on bling and fast cars?
When you should be aiming for the stars.
We all need to wake up and really think,
So in the well of ignorance we don't sink.

Through many teachers and schools,
Your given requisite skills and tools.
They help you to stand on your feet,
Dealing with trials of life & its heat.

Mastering sciences, R.E & History,
Et al awakening you to life's mystery.
Being educated is the real deal 'cool'
Staying focused & determined the rule.

Acquiring knowledge is a true treasure,
So precious its benefits haven't measure.
Learning knowledge is food for the brain,
Never is it a loss but always a self-gain.

There are many benefits of education,
Taking you to a higher & loftier station.
So with wisdom one just truly expresses,
The blessings to your thought processes.

Education for the future

Reflections we have as a guide & yardstick to lead the future way,
From the past to the present a gift not to be sent away.
From the knowledges & ways afforded to us today we can have greater success,
From books to educational institutes to places of learning we can't digress.

To ensure happiness, success & achievement without much sorrow,
We need the best in education for a brighter tomorrow.
The future cannot be a vision we see without exertion & hard working ways,
It requires strength & determination in the best so that today for tomorrow pays.

Educational enhancements have gone through change with new additions,
From thinkers & developers each who have their own visions.
Not investing in time for learning breeds ignorance & impediments,
Ensuring the void of ignorance is filled with knowledge is a compliment.

The best teachers & learners are like success stories through learning,
One takes from education to teach others qualifications often for earning.
Through time education has been a corner stone of successful civilisations,
The key to goodness & progress is useful knowledge in all nations.

Harmful knowledge & education is destruction to all societies,
It bridges nothing but barriers & dangers that lead to complexities.
Education therefore remains essential for future & present success,
If it is structures, taught & learnt lawfully well society will progress.

Educational successes are measured by what they produce by results,
The knowledge acquired is heritage the rest is for development of any faults.
The future is how we shape it & education is a key to its opening,
The door is success if what enters through is trained – 'The becoming'.

Islamic sciences have taught people skills of permanent retention,
Also being studious and showing adab (respect) & attention.
The greatest education begins and concludes with Allah's mention,
Granting you success in this world and the next & heavenly elevation.

Reflections on the times

We are living in testing times. Issues that span time are still prevalent and impending. Racism is one of these issues. The Prophet stated that a black person doesn't have superiority over a white person and vice versa except their piety. The Qur'an is clear on the issue of racism, and there is a stipulation on co-existence between various peoples and nations:

'And among His Signs is the creation of the heavens and the earth, and the variations in your languages and your colours, verily, in that there are signs for those who know.' (Qur'an, 30:22).

'O mankind, We created you from a single pair of a male and a female, and made you into tribes and nations that you may know each other (not that you despise each other). Verily, the most honoured of you in the sight of Allah is the most righteous of you…' (Qur'an, 49:13)

These beautiful verses acknowledge racial diversity and gender (male & female) as created by God.

Other impending issues are smoking and drugs which have been written about. Both are detrimental to one's health. The poems explore the medical and spiritual issues complimented with a poem think twice which is what we should do in the face of issues we encounter.

Not ashamed to be different is a poem that articulates the fact that you should not be ashamed of how you were born and moral issues you should adhere to. It is about appreciating the diversity God created in their natural states.

Tough Times

When things are getting rough,
feeling lonely like you get no love.
When things getting hard and dire,
trippin every corner not your desire.

Feeling kind of different & out of place,
your only crime was you another race.
Finding it hard when the bullies chase,
But hope and faith you got to embrace.

Being subject each day to another insult,
people telling you you're always at fault.
Feeling like you aint just good enough,
feel like a loser because you not tough.

People playing games with your mind,
Speaking words so unbelievably kind.
Their ignorance permeating you will find,
To the truth mate you should rather bind.

People still taunting you and your crew,
Say peeps 'we'd rather do the good we do!'
You don't need to be Mr or Miss Popularity,
you gotta know that life is real not fantasy.

Covered over with envy is the enemy,
sunken deep in the river of jealousy.
You need to believe in truth and integrity,
give away the ego my amigo and be so free.

Lets face it we can't win just feeling down,
gotta go out and win to achieve the crown.
You've got to believe deeply in yourself,
Seek Allah to aid you & the good to help.

There are people out there filled with hate,
anger and violence what a dreadful state.
But my friend you aint got time to wait,
gotta heal all the wounds before its late.

Racism – Goodbye, farewell!

An issue that shatters me deep down inside,
Its reality ever so detrimental you can't hide.
Where out of ignorance humans still divide,
Based on race others they taunt and deride.

In ridiculing God's gift of variety to cause pain.
Where in this is the winning, success and gain?
Seeing it manifest and unfold drives me insane,
Yet often we silently allow it & never complain.

Racism is premised on colour and not abilities,
A denial of equality and human complexities.
In a world where the ego people often please,
The rainbow of colour is greater with peace.

Derided on your culture, looks, race & figure,
Still often taunted by names like 'paki' or 'nigger',
But being the better person makes you bigger.
Its truth and justice that you want to deliver.

A case I'm thinking of is Malcolm X in point,
A former criminal was within the wrong joint.
He went to a prison cell for doing much crime,
With reflection he became Muslim in time.

Initially he joined a group filled with hate,
Slavery and persecution creating that state.
But the beautiful Hajj for him did liberate,
Seeing we're equal as one needing love not hate.

Reflecting and thinking no need for blame,
To Malik al Shabbaz he changed his name.
Didn't want the mind-set of racism a shame,
Blemishing the people through a nasty game,

No need for Pharaohs and Hitler's the brute.
The heart and mind racism does harm & loot.
We've got to remember God is the Truth,
Stand strongly firm and give racism the mute.

When God made us all, racists I ask you why?
Racism a blind ignorance let's say to it goodbye.
Beautiful diversity and equality you can't deny.
For this blessing no-one should ever have to cry.

Standing shoulder to shoulder as 1 human race,
Don't need a boring monotone world in its place.
Praying to be bestowed with heavenly grace,
The diversity of people with hearts embrace.

Racism – say no and taste the rainbow!

How can anyone conceivably be racist at all?
We are not bound by our colour or the nation, from which we came,
Internally we carry organs and the components making us the same.

Colours surround and fill this large world with intense beauty,
This rich myriad of all colours takes us on an amazing journey.
To alleviate ourselves from racism is thus really a shared duty,
So that we can change our world for more peace and serenity.

As the eyes do open with their hazel or blue lenses of light,
They glance at the world so coloured beautiful and bright.
We see colour in the alteration of day, night and the sunset.
So many shades in the seasons also, one just can't forget.

As the feet with multiple layers and colours touch ground,
The eyes see a myriad of flowers and scenery all around.
From the little and large birds we hear a humming sound,
So in your heart for colour and vibrancy a place must be found.

When the mouth relishes the taste of foods of all continents,
Colours, vibrancy and flavour become shared sentiments.
So when we mix and mingle in our mouths we experiment,
that the world is best shared, so no to racial impediment!

When we look at the worlds wonders we see people gaze,
Coming from all quarters, such amalgamation does amaze.
So no colour can deny the other and itself try to raise,
Together we all contribute best together for better ways.

If we can appreciate material objects with colours in our midst,
Then racism serves no basis beyond ignorance, so it we desist.
Because we are all equal and together in this world do exist,
So dialogue and appreciation we must try in life to persist.

With much blissful love, real care and ample affection,
We can always build with all of humanity a connection.
No barriers and walls are ever needed ever at this place,
Where equal opportunities should be whatever your race.

We're still having to tackle historic prejudices and hate,
But we all need to speak up now and not before its late.
We don't need to simply see the world in black or white,
But most importantly decipher between wrong and right.

We've seen so many past cruelties in the world unfold,
Our reactions are a speechless shock when we're told.
Though we can't go back in to the history of time,
We need to end now what is 'the repetition' past crime.

Let us appreciate the human rainbow and colourful rays,
Of humanity and diversity the better paths and ways.
To learn, share, and reflect as equals for better days,
We know in the long run equality to the heart pays.

From Africa, America, Europe to Asia & every continent,
Let's share wisdom and equality as loves true sentiment.
With hands and hearts we should always stand together,
and say to ignorant racism and genocide never, never!!

Smoking – It's harmful I'm not joking!

We've all heard about the addiction called smoking,
Biggest cause of preventable death, were not joking.
Each one is harmful and will slowly take your life,
Who after your death will support family, hub or wife?

It causes staining of your teeth and bad breath,
Its use causes after some time your eventual death.
Smoking is ruinous to lungs and causes lung cancer,
To life's purpose and quest this isn't the answer.

Each cigarette takes five minutes of your lifetime,
When God gave your life why commit this crime?
Give it up start now as your running out of time,
Amend your life and ways towards Allah sublime.

Smoking is often influenced by media & pressure,
But life is a sacred gift a real God given treasure.
Smoking for many is a daily & lifetime addiction,
Give it up today & have faith and firm conviction.

Smoking can also impact your ability to have a child,
By the Kiraman Katibeen the angels this is surely filed.
It can cause chronic obstructive pulmonary disease,
Only the makers these harmful effects it does please.

It is dangerous and contains in it carbon monoxide,
Why pay for ill health? Your intelligence they deride.
Remember you make the ultimate choice and decide,
None can the laws of your Creator ever override.

We know those who take it are likely to have a stroke,
Put out the fire it's a serious issue not a mere joke.
Smoking also causes a narrowing of your arteries,
Look cigarettes in the eye and say my clear enemies.

It can also lead to stomach ulcer or lungs emphysema,
Wake up my friend and stop being at loss a dreamer.
It contains the addictive substance known as nicotine,
So many fatalities through time it has clearly seen.

Smoking has no benefits or any correct type of purpose,
The images on packets should discourage no fuss.
For too long its money makers have kept you as a fool,
If something only causes harm why is it deemed cool?

Protect your life and family and give it to the bin,
Harming your life is deemed to be only an evident sin.
Take to health ways and with my Lord you'll win,
Remember taking care of your life & health is ever in.

Drugs – don't risk it!

You know that non-medicinal drugs are forbidden,
Why take them as nothing from Allah is hidden.
With drugs you know your life's end is very nigh,
So why fool yourself then in order to get on a high.

Life is endowed as sacred gift a God given treasure,
Drugs are harmful and endanger as the measure.
Don't give into false friends and social peer pressure,
Or even the lies on the packets for false pleasure.

They are hallucinogens and delude and mislead,
Stay to the real realms and in God's laws heed.
Be aware drugs consumption leads to addiction,
Endangering yourself & others is the devils mission.

Nothing is more hideous then intents of the dealers,
On our ill health and death making money – stealers!
Often if not they lead lives of much wealth & luxury,
Their entrenched greed should be obvious to see.

No legislation is greater than the one Allah gave,
The prophetic message & Qur'an from harm save.
Drugs often cloud and befog the human mind,
To your long term health they are solely unkind.

The addiction often to keep habit results in crime,
It leads to homelessness and imprisonment time.
It causes families break up, suffering & anguish,
Don't give into the complex money makers wish.

Cocaine damages the circulatory system and heart,
As do Heroin and ecstasy so don't cause life to part.
There is no type of benefit or actual personal gain,
Except from self-destruction & pain caused by cocaine.

An illegal substance that is addictive known as heroin,
Its consumption leads to death and coma a clear sin.
Leading to death due to dehydration is the drug Ecstasy,
Know that the giver is your murderer a clear enemy.

An effect & causing some mental illness is Cannabis,
Protect your mind & health and give this a clear miss.
Drug abuse can lead to HIV, infected blood and hepatitis.
Through syringe or injection leading you to your minus.

Avoid drugs seen as around like magic mushrooms,
They are illegal and drugs often kill you like bombs.
Life to you was given as a trust and as a sacred gift,
Protect your health and gain lawful wealth for an uplift.

Gangsters

Friend, do you want to be a gangster?
To your Lord you will have to answer.
Televised images your intelligence con,
Convincing you it's cool to be the don.

Easily influenced image perceptions,
Fight your ego and give up deceptions.
You thought you were acting very cool,
But the devil enjoys seeing you as a fool.

Convinced of your strength you abuse,
This immoral way you need to refuse.
Working out to appear to others tough,
When are you going to stop it's enough.

You want to be called the latest mafias,
The Prophetic examples were better as.
You have bowed into the peer pressure,
Don't give in and resort to this measure.

You lead your life like the mob tyrant,
False leadership to truth you are silent.
No independence you're another copycat,
Your convinced by your ego your all that.

You are leading a life resorting to crime,
But this life is a test make the most of time.
You've gained immoral types of addictions,
Your life is distant from prophetic missions.

I ask is a gangster one who takes drugs?
One who chills with the baddies the thugs?
Image creation you are driving fast cars,
Speeding cause's accidents and leave scars.

Some lifestyle is influenced by modern rap,
But the words just mislead you into a trap.
You go on a rampage out to have some fun,
Hands imprisoned to wrong holding a gun.

Far from reality stuck in fantasy & delusion,
Give it up friend Allah's path is the solution.
No matter how much you appear brave,
You'll be alone once you enter in your grave.

Islamophobia

Islamophobia is often found in stories & headline,
The Muslim ummah worldwide it wishes to undermine.
To isolation and exclusion Muslims it wishes to confine,
However their faith is rooted and emanates from divine.

Islamophobia permeates between the East and the West,
Those who endure it see how it is totally messed.
However this life wasn't made to be easy – it's a test.
Islamophobia is the game play of the devil at his behest.

The complete process emanates in total stupidity,
Born out of ignorance, vile, tyranny and enmity.
It harms the innocent and is aimed at their sanity,
It strikes at intelligence and is done out of profanity.

In modern times it has become the call of the far right,
Before it was the Jews – now Muslims in their sight.
It's a sick obsession that is taking on a new height,
They try to show prowess and use their money & might.

Many Muslims have endurance & suffer in silence,
They put up with insults, assaults and all types of violence.
They have to be strong and deal with it with resilience,
And have tawakkul since to Allah is their subservience.

Their faith & Prophet are depicted in ways derogatory,
Their foes speak in high places and low with false oratory.
Houses are damaged, violence erupts they have to worry,
But God will judge all in the end fairly – to Him is all glory.

Wars are proclaimed often against the Muslim veil,
Opportunities at work are closed & they ensure they fail.
They claim the clothing is oppression from God & male,
But on the path of Modesty Muslims freely adopt the veil.

Muslim women are discriminated for wearing Hijab,
Even more when they dress like Mary (r.a) & Nuns in Jilbab.
Various politicians shout many insults against the Nikab,
But Muslims vary and dress as above for love of their Rabb.

Islamophobia often has a heterophobic imposition,
Against the way of Lut (a.s) do they place a condition.
Muslims from Burma have endured from home eviction,
Only because their Muslim & have firm conviction.

Anders Breivik was a man rooted in the crusaders,
He harmed innocence and had the ideology of invaders.
Him and the new far right are staunch Muslim haters,
Beware the sickness of Islamophobia that often enters.

Think twice

Mate, how do you really want to be?
A friend a foe or just another enemy,
Unto yourself when you should be free.
      I ask you to make sure you think twice,
      Of the consequences you should realise,
      Don't wanna be the fool got to be wise.
In ignorance you were asleep now awaken,
To the righteous path that you'd forsaken.
On this deluded path so many lives taken.
      Hanging out and chilling with the thugs,
      When you can be spreading salams & hugs.
      Instead your killing yourself with drugs.
It's no good you taking them or dealing,
Resorting to criminal acts and stealing.
For the innocents affected I'm feeling.
      For alcohol and drugs they just cringe,
      So many accidents yet they still binge,
      asking for the death giving drug syringe.
I see the growth & rise of the addictions,
complimented with sentences & convictions.
Empty pockets & on streets from evictions.
      Daily routines the crews are thieving,
      Back at home mammas still grieving.
      Asking who are you peeps deceiving?
Are you just another wannabe gangster?
Living life like a wasted prankster.
When you forget Allah is your Master.
      They're fighting too many street wars,
      Their forgetting inside their own flaws.
      Closing for themselves heavens doors.
Fast like thunderbolts of lightening,
This mayhem and chaos is heightening.
With the fighting, wars and the rioting.
      It's the truth & reality your all masking,
      think of the ramifications is what i'm asking.
      You can change & amend its your akhira taxing.
From the pain & torment that your wreaking,
The record don't look good it needs tweeking.
The guidance is what you should be seeking.
      You know there's a better alternative,
      Repent, amend your ways & Allah will forgive,
      So that on a better path & way you can live.
As on Qiyamah account is for what you hath.
There is for us all laid a greater path,
Seek Allah's mercy, compassion not His wrath.
      All I can say people is please think twice,
      Life is too short I hope that you realize.
      Reflect and think about this sister's advice.

Not ashamed to be different

Not ashamed to be young and in education,
Geek calling & other names not worth mention.

Not ashamed to be wearing glasses and to look different to you,
They helped me to see during the days & nights through & through.

Not ashamed to be living in a caravan close by,
Poverty & travelling were not always the reason why.
Travellers explored the world like Alexander the great,
Zheng-He, Ibn Batutta & others that some may imitate.

Not ashamed to be a dual citizen or an immigrant,
We brought culture & shared values to compliment.
Complimenting all those things existing with vitality,
Food, clothes, culture, new designs with vibrancy.

Not ashamed to be short if it is how God made me,
I'm sure tall people may feel special equally in what they see.

Not ashamed to be a believer in Islam & its identity,
Religious values are part of history & present types of entity.

Not ashamed to be a person with born disability,
It's a test to strive & excel in other ways with given ability.

Not ashamed to be concerned about the world some find it boring,
It's amazing to reflect from the dark night to the bright morning.

Not ashamed to be a lover of good in the face of anarchy,
Since immorality, tyranny and injustice are from the enemy.

Not ashamed to be hard working, studious and learning,
It will aid me in life, those around me & in my earning.

Not ashamed to care for bullying in different locations,
Today it's you, tomorrow others as the villains create complications.

Not ashamed to worry & weep when an innocent soul dies,
Ideally they want you to keep strong & endeavour to be goodies.

Not ashamed to be created either white, brown or black,
It remains a reason to understand, appreciate & not attack.

Not ashamed to be a thinker in my own right,
& see things in a new form or complex light.

Others

Appreciation, gratitude and thanking of others are positive values of humility and goodness that acknowledge Allah and others. The Prophet (pbuh) said:

"He who does not thank the people is not thankful to Allah." (Abu Dawud)

Praising and glorifying God are signs of gratitude to Allah. He desires that we're grateful to others.

Caring about others is encouraged in the Qur'an and Sunnah. Tears is a poem about that support. We should be shoulders to lean on (not literally) for others.

The world of trials is about the trials we are enduring and facing.

Healing is about acknowledging the difficulties people endure.

Tears

As I glanced at you I saw that tear slowly
fall down your soft and tender face,
It reminded me of human fervour to
accomplish the success of the human race.

Don't let those tears of feelings and love
and emotion touch the ground of earth,
You are very precious no matter what is
Said God knows your true real worth.

Your tears I would rather you give to in
my hands to absorb and empathise,
That your happiness is slowly lost into
my heart as your feelings I realise.

Your tears are not some type of
meaningless droplets that fall with disgrace,
Your tears are symbolic of human love
and continual need of divine grace.

So don't cry my friend alone as your
tear carries with it a million words,
Like the roaming and continual
tweeting and flying beautiful little birds.

So herald yourself not to the limit of
emotion inexpressible in tone,
As to you I share my shoulder and so
do not fear as you are not alone.

Take no shame in tears that fall as they
manifest human nature and style,
Please be reconciled in forgiveness as
your alternative, so again do smile.

Tears are surely not fanciful and serve
as an expression where words are lost,
But recognise their precious worth for
which they can't be replaced by cost.

So fear not friend and be at peace &
wipe away those tears of anguish,
As your supporting pillar always
your happiness always is my wish.

Those tears that you have cried,
Entrusted to me I will confide.
Standing there just by your side,
Collecting these gems you cried.

Gratitude

We need so much gratitude & love,
Knowing we be blessed by God above.
Shining light to your life illuminating,
Grace and faith is truly liberating.

Beauty of the heart is always best,
with every heart beat your blessed.
Praise and glorify The unique Maker,
designed and fashioned by the Creator.

Time don't be wasted when it's a blessing,
We know changes inevitable so no messing.
Open hearts and minds you'll see the truth,
It's always in to be good, never uncouth.

Don't despair my friend aim high don't stop,
see yourself on heaven's score board at the top.
Time is ticking and we know it gets harder,
but it's the test of life that's the real starter.

Give and don't worry we got to share,
for the orphaned and weak we must care.
No need for corners and places to hide,
make amends and know Allah's by your side.

Keep the rhythmic peace and sing its song,
we know through thick & thin gotta be strong.

An ode of appreciation

How imbued & how fulfilled we feel when appreciated,
So deep in the heart where it's special - God keeps you liberated.
How much do we really appreciate others around us who may be different to us,
Still uniquely equal & no different essentially but it's the story thus.
To appreciate every little soul God brought into the world unique,
Every fingerprint & hair individual to you so you can't be bleak.
Always look at the child & respect the soul God breathed into it,
Unique in every way & irreplaceable as God designed your wit.
For you to use your wit to appreciate a higher talent that made you & everything,
So when you see people in whatever shape & form it will make you a better something.
The blind friend wants appreciation like everybody else out there,
To be more responsible & helpful is a blessing so be aware.
Dangers can always lurk around you even if you can see,
But you cannot see how sweet & appreciative & content of heart the blind maybe.
The one who cannot walk suffering from paralysis severe,
Still acknowledges the life within & appreciates Allah (SWT) most dear.
The one who cannot hear in their sight is sense of visual understanding,
Conceptualising by image as though the images speak on their own behalf.
Through a new development from each image like the talking hands,
From sign language the language that they see & live with as life demands.
Also, as with the others they appreciate God for great strength to be alive,
With God's blessing all of them equal yet unique have reasons to thrive.

Thank you
Thank you to the heroes of everyday,
For spending and exerting time for all,
Working for enhancement in every way.
Heeding and implementing a divine call.

Thank you to the parents who care,
Bringing up miracles one comprehends,
With kindness & love they often share.
Helping dependents become independents.

Thank you to those who work in health,
Aiding and healing wounds and many scars.
Knowing protecting body & mind is wealth,
Their dedication shows their shining stars.

Thank you to those doctors healing pain,
Giving solutions and much needed advice.
Helping the sick and needy over again,
Their good exertions one should realise.

Thank you to the teachers imparting good,
Teaching knowledge & much information,
Carrying on the legacy one really should.
Becoming filled with heartily illumination.

Thank you to those who work in Charity,
Working through war & disastrous extremes.
Poverty & impoverishment given much clarity,
Their beneficiaries able to realize their dreams.

Thank you to those peeps who clean the earth,
Freshening and preserving the world's beauty,
Knowing custodianship a role given at birth.
Completing a beneficial and good duty.

Thank you to those friends always there,
Protecting you from all types of wrong.
Who show no matter what they truly care,
Always keeping you at all odds strong.

Thank you to those who remind you of Allah,
Blessing your life with dhikr and success.
Uniting all people by calling you to salah,
Help you change to know that Allah does bless.

Thank you to the great people of the past,
Who taught wisdom, knowledge and all good.
Whose legacies brought success and will last,
Left you the seeds of growth so you also would.

Thank you to Allah the Merciful Creator,
Who gave us all the others with much love.
Who sent us miracles & the final liberator.
& sent many divine blessings from high above.

Healing

I see another sad wound & another scratch,
Is it another bad fight or another match?
      It's another trial & another daily patch,
      You are another victim of a criminal catch.
For countless days so many tears cried,
You felt you were the only one here tried,
      But on this journey I remain on your side,
      Let us unite firmly and never ever divide.
In you this trust I will have to confide,
Remain steadfast and Allah's laws abide.
      So much pain you feel introverted and tired,
      Chained in this sea of injustice so wide.
Remember the Qur'an is your guide,
From Allah no one can ever, ever hide.
      I know the pain & wounds your feeling,
      Death of innocence your daily grieving.
Whilst the enemy carried on deceiving,
Leaving wounds so painfully seething.
      Don't give up with love there's healing,
      With faith in Allah we keep on believing.
Recount his mercies were all receiving,
For our hearts and minds faith is freeing.
      Remember Allah is truly the All-Seeing,
      The Creator of every human & being.
Pain, pain don't let it be your final end,
As these words of solace I heartily send.
      With words of heart most truly meant,
      A gift for keeping not temporarily leant.
I hope the transgressors can repent,
Since death is ever upon us imminent.
      My friend your innocence is clearly evident,
      We can all change just try this element.
A little change to sadaqah is well spent,
A gesture of goodness a real sentiment.
      Out of anguish & pain you would groan.
      But it was difficult for you not to moan.
Not in the world are any of us here alone,
Fighting with so many hearts like stone.
      Enveloping an injustice it is really wrong,
      We can't give up we need to be strong.
To Allah we return & to Him we belong,
On a journey of life if it is short or long.
      Winds of injustice far away they're blown,
      With remembrance of Allah in every tone.
In the skies of freedom we have flown,
By love of Allah we have truly shown.
      Tears wiped and healing manifest our own,
      From the light of mercy that's truly shone.
Hence every wound we clear with love,
Invoking the divine blessings from above.
      Praise Allah and you will be truly healed,
      His mercy limitless for us to be believed.

The world of trials

Great trials & tests we daily endure,
       Sabr & Iman remain the solution & cure.
For a surety we won't always exist,
       Temptations and injustices we must resist.
Dreams & hopes often shattered,
       Many lives broke & families scattered.
Yet we live with 'it's all about just me'
       Yet enslaved in systems of thought, be free.
Time is an asset use it in every way,
       Let our actions compliment what we say.
We can all really collectively succeed,
       So long as were not subdued in greed.
Count your blessings from Allah,
       Glorify Him with praises in every salah.
Remember He knows all the truth,
       Even when we're silenced and mute.
Criticisms and insults are commonplace,
       From the people who wish only to disgrace.
This vicious circle with taqwa we can erase,
       Remember it is a long trial and difficult phase.
Hold strong as the tides are now arising,
       Subdued in a sleep the realities were realising.
On faith there can't be compromising,
       Even if that sincerity the deniers are despising.
Those who wish to hinder wish wrong,
       But to Allah we all do collectively belong.
With Tawwakul we must all remain strong.
       This trial is strenuous and very, very long.
Unity is key and a way to overcome,
       As from one a collective our minds become.
In poverty or richness no distinction,
       We believe in the haqiqat & not in fiction.
Use every second upon you entrusted,
       With injustice we must fully be disgusted.
Wrong we know cannot ever be right,
       We must fill these voids with spiritual light.
Giving up we know is the easiest route,
       Never bow down in the face of those brute.
Unite man, woman, old and the youth,
       Stand strong and firm on the path of truth.

The Sojourners Journey

Awakening upon the journey is highly required,
Full exertion & focus if it is Allah (SWT) we desired.
Journey not to be stolen or any way taken or broken,
It's one requiring affirmation, action & what's spoken.
The destiny is to the greatest whose blessings are immense,
Who gave you the blessings within yourself such as sense?
Five senses for direction in order to experience life,
Life for the benefit of self and others who have strife.
The journey requires equipping in order to fully succeed,
To follow divine law and the righteous and God you heed.
The excuses of all will be many for difficulties may arise,
Some take the truth in mock, others the way they despise.
The way is not to be cheated since it would only fail,
It is gainful for the steadfast whether male or female.
With the right tools the best way in life can be built,
Leading life in the spiritual path will guide & keep fulfilled.
My Lord is the one to seek as one travels to success,
In devotion, worship and remembrance this express.
To guide us to Jannah & the highest success each day,
From the blessings that my Lord gave to us on the way.
Many may come on the journey of different walks and ways,
They may follow the straightway or incorrectly their own ways.
The way requires knowledge obtained only through learning,
Since lawfulness is vital if it is closeness to Allah that you're yearning.
Many false ideologies and ways make claim to the truth,
It is better to be steadfast so that you win in old age & youth.
True success is with the One whom no knowledge of all is hidden,
Who gives the boundaries of what is lawful and forbidden.
Your blessings that are yours already are present look inside,
By the Creator the bounties & blessings your skin does hide.
Be surprised when Millions & billions are the riches within,
Acknowledge God and be grateful to God & each will win.
Be sincere and Ishq of my Lord & His Prophet will guide,
With intentions the route of the way will unite not divide.
Remember that since my Lord knows what is truly best,
Goodness is the key to success in the life's given test.

The Awakenings

Reflection, introspection were all awakening,
Sleeping, enveloping exhaustion were all hating.
Lethargic from energy losses & take outs,
Questionable imbalances & strange pass outs.
It's time to awaken from a deep sleeping mode,
On the backs of humans a burdensome load.
Awakening, eyes open & minds & hearts aware,
Of everything around you, time losses beware.
Awakening from the dark nights to the bright days,
All grown up now time for maturity – no game plays.

Awakening from forsaking things that make you good,
Too much pre-existing prejudice to get you misunderstood.
Time costing and wasted its heavy like other things too,
Unhealthy to life opportunities for the future you.
Awakening there's too much in the world to reflect,
United action for peace & world change we need to react.
Time losses can't be rewinded the past remains the past,
Speed up with the time wasting thief getting fast.
Awakening power struggles have the world subdued,
World peace & sharing, they all need to be clued.

Awakening from good hating will get you on a high,
A high of morality & reflection don't believe the lie.
Stay constant and acutely aware of your persons & beings,
Times are envied so be prepared for happiness and grieving's.
Awakening different ideas fast floating like in space,
Remember upon this earth temporary is your place.
Eyes for seeing, minds for thinking & hearts for love,
Floating like a swan or flying as gently as a dove.
Like the world around you all need to remain aware,
That dangers exist all the time - don't walk into the lair.

Remembrance & Supplication

Muslims believe that Allah is the answerer of supplications. There are many prayers in the Qur'an. The prophet left various invocations for his followers for a variety of things. Many of these prayers or duas (supplications) are like a conversation between the believer and God. Allah likes to hear His servants supplicate. Some supplications are answered in this world and some in the next.

An example of a supplication in the Qur'an is that of Musa (a.s) when he was in difficulty. "My Lord, put my heart at peace for me and make my task easy for me and remove the knot from my tongue, that they may understand my speech." (Qur'an 20:25,26,27,28)

Abu Hurairah (r.a) narrated that Allah's Messenger (pbuh) said: 'In the last third of every night our Rabb (Cherisher and Sustainer) (Allah (SWT)) descends to the lowermost heaven and says; "Who is calling Me, so that I may answer him? Who is asking Me so that may I grant him? Who is seeking forgiveness from Me so that I may forgive him?."' [Sahih al-Bukhari, Hadith Qudsi]

Muslims believe Allah is Al-Razzaq (The Provider) as he gives provision to His creation and he forgives the supplicator by their intent he is At-Tawwab (Acceptor of Repentance). They also believe He is Al-Ghafur (The Forgiving) so they direct their supplications to Him.

The Angels come to the gatherings where Allah's name is mentioned. Remembrance or Zikr as it is called binds the believer to Allah.

Remembrance

Through morning & night seek the blessings of remembrance,
To develop your faith, & your journey it will only enhance.
Remembrance & gratitude with countless praises,
Since God created you and let you live in various places.
Lofty positions develop through the purest of intent,
With those who are faithful with righteous sentiment.
Faith is not lost since it is already fully complete,
Open for hidayah by the intentioned well – the faithful seat.
Zikr develops the faith for the individuals to succeed,
If the sojourner the path God decreed will heed.
Half & Half is a test not the representation when wrong,
Remembrance & acknowledgement is the best to remain strong.
Those who are righteous in Zikr may reach state of Ihsan,
It requires prayer, piety, Taqwa and uncompromising iman.
Praise him every day and the time you receive something,
He created you and He is free of want of anything.

A Muslim Dua (Supplication)

My Lord make us righteous and God fearing,
You know our intentions you're the All-Hearing.
Make us people of Ibadah and repentance,
Grant us Jannah not hell and its sentence.

My Lord make us people of firm gratitude,
Make us humble with the correct attitude.
Oh Al-Ghafur forgive us our mistakes & sins,
Make us amongst the righteous 'ins wal jinns'.

Oh Al-Hakim make us intelligent and wise,
Those who yearn for your love & the devil despise.
Make us of those who follow the siddiqeen,
Make us successful upon Islam the final deen.

Oh Al-Aleem make us people of knowledge,
Grant us success in school, university & college.
Oh An-Nur grant us continual spiritual light,
Make us those who acknowledge your Might.

Oh Allah the one with 99 beautiful names,
Protect us from Iblis and his devious games.
Make us firm on the path of monotheism,
Protect us like the Prophets from polytheism.

Oh As-Sami make us Saliheen Oh Al-Baseer,
Make us people of Taqwa with your love & fear.
Make us of those who will be given shade,
Protect us from the sins which you forbade.

Oh As-Salam grant the Ummah much peace,
Take us out of difficulty and grant us ease.
Make us sincere & you whom we wish to please,
Make us humble as we prostrate upon our knees.

Protect us from the smouldering fire of sijjeen,
Make us those who rise up to the gift of illiyin.
Grant us Islam's success as your chosen deen,
Make us generous and kind and not mean.

Make us of those who live and die on Shahadah,
Make us of those who maintain good and amanah.
Make us of those who daily pray their full salah,
Make us of those obedient & loved by Allah.

Ameen

Dua

May Allah guide me to what is right,

May Allah endow me with spiritual light,

May Allah give me the truth in what I write,

May Allah give me spirituality in my sight,

May Allah make me reflect through foresight,

May Allah help me in my struggles & fight,

May Allah give me strong iman day & night,

May Allah guide me to a future bright.

Ameen

Spiritually fulfilled conclusion

Spiritually fulfilled in life to be complete,
Try to work arduously and not compete.
Attain love of God and the devil defeat,
Remember God has the mightiest seat.

Fulfilled and enlightened by al-Islam,
With Sunnah and Qur'an Allah's Kalam.
Empowering nur ala nur still amazes,
Gratitude of God's countless graces.

Inside Firm iman internal and external,
To the cold it is warm heat and thermal.
Nourishing the body, soul and heart,
Do say the bismillah before you start.

Fulfilment in completion of ½ your deen,
Taqwa in the rest where you've been.
Ihsan envelops with truth the believer,
Protection & guard against the deceiver.

Following the five pillars brings blessing,
Saying the Shahadah is the attesting.
Salah humbly brings you close to God,
Hajj unifies all and no-one is left odd.

You need to purify your intent & soul,
Travel with the Teachers for your goal.
Those in faith who guide on the path,
Blessed by divine mercy not God's wrath.

Spiritually fulfilled like a precious gem,
Member of the Ummah to be of them.
To meet with the beloved of the nation
Teaching and education his occupation,

Yearning to be close to Allah the Almighty,
He favours those who love Him from piety.
It suffices with what He gave in our quest,
To us He sent to emulate the Prophet the best.

Spiritually fulfilled by this faith is the way,
Each is tested in dunya every single day.
The map to success will give you treasure,
Jannah for the upright from God's measure.

Appendix 1

Books quoted from:

Qur'an (various quotes)

Islam The Natural Way, Abdul Wahid Hamid, Mels 1989

Kitab Ash-Shifa, Qadi 'Iyad Ibn Musa al-Yashubi, Translated. Aisha Abdarrahman Bewley), 1999,

The wives of the Prophet Muhammad (s.a.w), Ahmad Thompson

Mathnawi by Jalaluddin Rumi Book III & Book IV

Ibn Hajar Al-Isaba

Hadith quotes found in topical books – hadiths are still quoted with hadith collector

Hadith, Bukhari

Hadith, Muslim

Imam Nawawi Forty Hadith (Hadith2)

Hadith, Tirmidhi

Hadith, Adh-Dhahabhi

Hadith, Tabari & Jami

Hadith Ibn Hanbal

Hadith, Nasa'i

Hadith, Abu Dawud

Appendix 2

The 99 names of Allah

Al-Khaliq (The Creator)
As-Sabur (The Forbearing)
Al-Hakim (The Wise)
Al-Mu'id (The Restorer)
Al-Badi (The Originator)
Al-Musawwir (The Shaper)
Ar-Rafi (The Exalter)
Al-Wahhab (The Bestower)
Al-Wakil (The Trustee)
Al-Qahhar (The Dominant)
Al-Jabbar (The Irresistible)
Al-Mu'izz (The Honourer)
Al-Quddus (The Holy)
Al-Muqaddim (The Bringer Forward)
Al-Haleem (The Kindly)
Al-Mumit (The giver of death)
Al-Wajid (The self-reliant)
Al-Matin (The Firm)
Dhul-Jalal Wal Ikram (The Lord of Majesty & Generosity)
Al-Muntaqim (The Avenger)
Al-Baqi (The Everlasting)
Al-Ghani (The Self-sufficient)
As-Salam (The All-Peace)
Ar-Rafi (The Exalter)
Al-Muqit (The Maintainer)
Al-Aliy (The Sublime)
Al-Azim (The Great One)
Al-Adl (The Just)
Al-Wasi (The All-Embracing)
Al-Mubdi (The Founder)
Al-Qawi (The Strong)
Malik ul Mulk (The possessor of the Kingdom)
Ar-Rashid (The Guide)
Al-Majeed (The Glorious)

Al-Malik (The Sovereign)
Az-Zahir (The Evident)
Al-Karim (The Generous)
Al-Hakam (The Judge)
Al-Majid (The Glorious)
Al-Muqtadir (The Prevailer)
Al-Mujib (The Responsive)
At-Tawwab (The Acceptor of Repentance)
Al-Mudhill (The Abaser)
Al-Mutakabir (The Superb)
Al-Barr (The Benificent)
Al-Muhaymin (The Protector)
Al-Muta'ali (The self-exalted)
Ar-Rahim (IThe Merciful)
Ar-Razzaq (the Provider)
Al-Muqsit (The Just)
As-Samad (The Eternal)
Al-Batin (The Inner)

Al-Barr (The Benificent)
An-Nafi (The Propitious)
Al-Bari (The Maker)
Al-Rahman (The Compassionate)
Al-Qabid (The Seizer)
Al-Hafiz (The Guardian)
Ash-Shakur (The Appreciative)
Al-Khabir (The Aware)
Al-Baith (The Resurrector)
Al-Jalil (The Glorious)
Al-Muhsi (The Counter)
Al-Qadir (The Capable)

Al-Warith (The Inheritor)
Al-Muhyi (The Giver of life)

An-Nur (The Light)
Al-Akhir (The Last)
Al-Khafid (The Abaser)
Al-Hadi (The Guide)
Al-Wahid (The One)
As-Sami (The All-Hearing)
Ar-Raqib (The Watchful)

Al-Ghaffar (The Forgiving)
Al-Mu'akhkhir (The Delayer)
Al-Aziz (The Mighty)
Al-Mumin (Giver of Peace)
Al-Wali (The Protector)
Al-Aleem (The All-Knowing)
Al-Haqq (The Truth)
Ash-Shahid (The Witness)
Al-Ahad (The One)
Al-Qayyum (The Self-subsistent)
Al-Afuw (The Supreme Pardoner)
Ad-Dar (The Distressor)
Al-Mughni (The Enricher)
Al-Jami (The Gatherer)
Al-Basir (The All-Seeing)
Al-Fattah (The Opener)
Al-Kabir (The Great)
Al-Ghafur (The Pardoner)
Al-Latif (The Gracious)
Al-Wadud (The Loving)
Al-Hasib (The Reckoner)
Al-Hamid (The Praiseworthy)
Al-Hayy (The Living)
Al-Rauf (The Gentle)
Al-Mani (The Preventor)
Al-Waliy (The Patron)

Glossary

Note: generally where explanations are offered in brackets in the book I have not added most of them in the glossary

A
Abase – to lower something down
Aberration – oddness and unusual
Abstaining – keeping away from
Abu Huraira (r.a) – Companion of Prophet
Accolades - honours, prayers, awards and tributes
Acquisition – what you acquire or gain
Adhan – Muslim call to prayer
Akhi - brother
Akhira – life after death
Alhamdulillah – all Praise be to Allah
Al-Quds – Holy city of Jerusalem
Amal – actions or behaviour
Amalgamated – brought together & mixed
Amalgamation - mixture
Amanah – trust
Ambiya – the Prophets
Amity – peace & harmony
Angels - beings made of light
Antagonist – against something
Antagonism – dislike, ill-feeling or hate towards
Annihilation – wiping out & extermination
Antithesis – the opposite
Anxiety – mental state of mind, impatience
Aqiqah – Muslim birth ceremony
Arduously – very hard
Articulation - expression
Ascended – go up
Asma ul Husna – 99 names of Allah
Assigned – task given to
Assiya (r.a) – the wife of Pharaoh
Aql - intellect
Aura – atmosphere
Azrail – Angel of death

B
Barricaded – covered, blocked and secured
Barzakh – state of waiting in grave
Beget – to give birth to
Begotten – born from
Benefactor – sponsor or supporter
Benevolence – God's kindness
Bequeath – will, donate to or confer
Bereft – grieve or mourn
Bestows – gives, confers, donates
Blemish – imperfection, mark or stain

Blossoming - growing
Blissful – heavenly, perfect, ideal
Brute – bully or tyrant
Bukhari – famous collector of hadith
Buraq – flying creature the Prophet rode on the night journey

C
Carnage – destruction of
Cave Hira – cave Prophet received revelation in
Cessation – the end
Cicumambulate – to go around
Clout – influence or power
Cognisant – aware of
Cohesion – unity and togetherness
Commemoration – to remember
Compassionate - kind, caring shows compassion (love)
Conceive – the fertilisation of egg and sperm
Confers – gives to others, delegate
Connive - plot, schemes & conspires
Contingent – dependent
Covetousness – desiring the belongings of others

D
Dairdayl – angels that look for people in gatherings.
Dawud (a.s) – Prophet & messenger of Allah
Deciphering – to decide and choose from
Detriment - to your own loss or damage
Devotedly - loyally and faithfully
Discretion – to keep to self
Dispelled – dismissed from
Divine – from God & holy
Demeans – to put down
Derision - mockery, contempt and ridicule
Derogatory - insulting and offensive
Destiny – fate and future
Dominates – goes above a thing/s or person/s
Dunya – the worldly life
Dutiful – to do something as asked

E
Egalitarianism – equality
Effaced – got rid of
Elevates –to place in a higher position

Elevation – placed in higher position
Eliminate – to get rid of
Elimination – gotten rid of
Emanates – comes from
Emanation – came from
Emancipation - freedom
Embedded – ingrained in
Emblems – symbols and signs
Embolden – encourage, inspire & bolster
Empowered – sanctioned or given strength in something
Emulation – to follow example of
Encapsulates – summarises and captures
Encompasses – to be covered or surrounded by
Enhancement – to boost or heighten
Enlightened – reaching an illumined position
Eschatology – study of the things at the end of time
Exorbitant - high
Exploitation – the process to exploit or unfairly take advantage of

F
Fatalism – belief you have no free-will or choice
Fallacy – contradiction or mistake
Finite – limited nature
Flamboyant - showy, colourful and loud
Foreknowledge – to know before something is to happen
Fragmentation – broken and divided
Furqan – The Criterion

G
Glorification – To praise something
Grace – blessings from God
Grandeur – majesty and dignity
Goyim – Hebrew for non-Jew

H
Hadith – sayings of the Prophet Muhammad (p.b.u.h)
Hajj - Pilgrimage
Hamal'at al Arsh – Angels that carry the throne
Haqiqat – the truth
Hidayah – guidance
Hijab – the head scarf worn by Muslim women
Hypothetico deductive method – the scientific method

I
Ibadah - worship
Ibn Batutta – Muslim traveller and travelogue writer
Ibrahim (a.s) – Abraham (p.b.u.h) prophet of God
Idolatry – worhips of created gods i.e. idols
Iftar – opening of the fast
Ihsan – state of worship to see God or know He sees you
illiyin – part of heaven
Illumination – to be given light of something
Ilm – knowledge
Iman – faith also refers to articles of faith
Iman ay Mufassal – prayer that outlines six beliefs
Immanent – God is close to us
Imbue – fills
Immaculately - perfectly
Immorality – something wrong or sinful
Impermissible – not allowed
Imperatively – importantly
Impoverishment – poverty, lacking & failure
Infallible – unchanged and pure
Infatuated – smitten or love-sick
Infinite – has no limit or beginning or end
Injil – the Gospel given to Jesus (p.b.u.h)
Inception – the beginning
Insinuation – to imply something
Ins wal jinns – humans and jinn
Intricacies – it's minuet details
Intrinsically – inherently or internally
Introspection – self reflection
Isa (a.s) – Prophet Jesus (p.b.u.h)
Ishq - love
Islam – Religion of Muslims also refers to 5 pillars
Islamophobia – hatred or fear of Islam
Israfil – Angel that blows horn to commence the end of time
Isra wal Miraj – The prophet's night journey

J
Jannah - heaven
Jibrail – Angel that gives messages from God to messengers.
Jilbab – outer dress and garment worn by Muslim women
Jinn- beings made out of smokeless fire
Jubilation - celebrations

K
Kab'ah – House of God in Mecca
Kalam – speech
Kawthar – river in heaven whiter than milk and sweeter than honey
Khutba al Hajja – The prophet's farewell sermon
Kiraman Katibeen – angels on shoulders that write your deeds

L
Lahw ul Mahfuz – preserved tablet containing revelation.
LEDC – less economically developed countries
Lethargic - tired, lazy or exhausted
Lofty – high
Lut (a.s) – the Prophet Lot (p.b.u.h)

M
Magnitude - extent
Malik – Angel in charge of hell
Manifestation - expression, display and appearance
Mariam (r.a) – the mother of Jesus (p.b.u.h)
Maqam – station or position
Mashallah – what God Wills
Mikail – Angel
Miracle – divine act breaking laws of nature
Mizan – balance where deeds will be weighed
Messengers – Prophets given revelation
Monotheism – belief in one God
Morality – principles of right or wrong
Muallim – the teacher – referring to the Prophet
Mujiza – miracle performed by a prophet
Mumin - believer
Mumineen - believers
Munkar & Nakir – Angels that question in the grave
Musa (a.s) – the prophet Moses (p.b.u.h)
Muslim – scholar and name of hadith collector

N
Nafs – ego
Naseeha - advice
Nawawi – Imam and scholar famous for hadith collection
Nikab – the face covering worn by Muslim women
Nikkah - the event marking signing of marriage contract
Niyyah - intention
Nur - light

O
Obedient – does as is asked – obeys
Obligation - duty
Obsolete – empty
Oratory – discussion & speech-making
Ordained - something destined that is going to happen
Ordinances - orders and decrees

P
Perennial – important
Permeating – surrounding you
Perpetrated – committed and planned against
Persecution – oppression and ill-treatment
Pivotal – essential
Polytheism – belief in many gods
Postulates – making a point
Premise – starting point
Profanity – blasphemy, sacrilege & disrespect
Prognosis - the diagnosis
Prophesize – Prophet foretelling the future
Proponent - the one in favour of or proposer
Prosecution – those at a trial that take action
Protagonist – in favour of something
Provision – providing with

Q
Qadr – divine destiny
Qisas al Ambiya – stories of the Prophets
Quintessentially - essentially
Qur'an – Muslim holy book

R
Ramifications – the results or consequences of
Reciprocated - shared
Recompense – reward and repayment
Regression – going backwards
Reminiscent – meaningful and remembrance of
Resonated – echoed or vibrated
Revelation – something revealed by God
Rejuvenated – revitalised, recharged and strengthened
Resonates - echoes and vibrates
Revitalisation – reborn, refreshed and renewed
Ridwan - Angel
Rife - difficulty

S

Salah – prayer 5 times a day
Salient - important
Saliheen – holy and pious
Sahaba – companions of Muhammad (p.b.u.h)
Sanctimoniously - piously
Sanctuary – place of rest and protection
Salutations - praise and greetiings
Satan – the devil also called iblis
Sawm – fasting in Ramadan
Schism – to break away from the original
Sehri – morning time of meal before fast closes
Sentimental – important, emotional
Sentiments – feelings of a kind
Serenity – peace
Servitude – serving and owned to other
Shahadah – declaration of faith
Shaheed – martyr, someone who dies for Islam
Shifa - healing
Shirk – association of partners with God
Shukr – gratitude and appreciation
Siddiqeen - the truthful
Sijjin - hell
Sirat – bridge to cross over to receive heaven
Sojourner - traveller
Sovereign - Kingly
Spiritual contemplation – religious reflection
Smouldering – blazing and burning fire
Stagnation – lagging behind or backwards
Subdued – to be taken over
Subhanallah – Glory be to Allah
Subjectivity – based on opinion not fact
Sublime – beautiful and inspiring
Submission - obedience to
Submit - to give in and do as has been asked/tasked
Subordinate – to submit to and be subservient towards
Subsists – exists and lives
Suhuf – revelation given to Ibrahim (a.s)
Summation – summary
Summations – summaries of
Sunnah – example of the prophet
Surah – part of the Qur'an

T

Talbiyah – prayer read during Hajj (pilgrimage)
Taqwa – God consciousness
Tawhid – oneness of Allah
Tawaakul – put trust in Allah
Tentatively – cautiously
Testification – to testify and express belief in something
Theodicy – defending the attributes of the of classical Theism from problem of evil
Torah – Holy book revealed to Musa (a.s)
Tormentors – those that oppress and harm
Transcends – above and beyond limit
Transcendent – God is above and beyond us
Transmission – from one person to the other
Tranquillity – peace
Transgressors – those who do wrong beyond limit
Traverse – to go on that path
Tribulations - tests and trials of difficulty

U

Ukhti – sister
Ummah – Muslim community
Unanimity – an agreement
Uswutun husna – beautiful character

V

Vendettas – campaigns, feuds and wars

W

Wali – friend
Wallah – by God
Wrath – anger

Y

Yaqeen – have faith in
Yaqub (a.s) – the prophet Jacob (p.b.u.h)
Yawm ul Qiyamah – Day of judgement
Yusuf (a.s) – the prophet Joseph (p.b.u.h)

Z

Zabaniyah – angels that punish in hell
Zakah – almsgiving or compulsory charity
Zheng-He – Chinese Muslim traveller
Zikr – remembrance of Allah
Zulm – oppression and injustice

Abbreviations

(SWT) Subhana Wa Taala
(SAW) Sallallahu wa aiahi wa salam (p.b.u.h)
(a.s) peace be upon him/her
(p.b.u.h) peace be upon him

(r.a) may God be pleased with him/her

About the author

Shaista Hussain was born in Birmingham in 1982. She graduated from the University of Birmingham with a degree in Intercultural Studies. She has a P.G.C.E in Religious Education from the same University and is a qualified teacher of Religious Education who has taught for a few years. She has a Master's in Education obtained from the aforementioned university. She is also a qualified mentor and also qualified as a Life Coach. She has written poetry since a young age and one of her first poems 'What is the point of Racism?' was submitted to the International Society of Poetry. She is a writer who writes in various styles and for various audiences – watch this space!

About the book

Spiritually fulfilled is a collection of over 100 poems on a multiplicity of themes on Islam as well as generic and topical interest in relation to Islam and other perennial issues. It deals with deep moral and relevant issues and also contains theology through poetry. The book is ideal to help Muslims and Non-Muslims to increase in their knowledge of Islam. It is useful also to the student whether at secondary, college or university. It is an informative book through poetry with introductory pages on most sections. It will help the reader on the odyssey of learning, understanding and comprehending about Islam. The poems include: The 99 names of Allah, Muhammad (p.b.u.h) A mercy to mankind, The veil, The child and the sages – reflective help from the wise, God's existence, Racism, Palestine, Smoking, Drugs & Gangsters.